The Tide
is Turning

The Tide
is Turning

Terry Virgo

New Wine Press

New Wine Ministries
PO Box 17
Chichester
West Sussex
United Kingdom
PO19 2AW

Fully revised and updated from the book *Men of Destiny*.

ISBN 1–903725–74–7

Typeset by CRB Associates, Reepham, Norfolk
Cover design by CCD, www.ccdgroup.co.uk
Printed in Malta

Contents

CHAPTER 1

The Turning Tide

We need visionaries, tough fighters and tenacious builders if we are going to see the gospel succeed in our generation and build strong churches that engage with our contemporary culture and bring in the kingdom of God.

Against the backdrop of advancing secularism and rampant atheism we see churches closing on all sides, particularly in the West, where Christianity is often regarded as old hat, quaint and irrelevant. Strangely, at the same time it is evident that new churches are springing up everywhere. Pentecostalism is sweeping the world and gaining phenomenal numbers. The so-called "charismatic movement" which broke out in the 1960s and overflowed into most of the historic denominations has also had extraordinary impact, though not without controversy.

God promised, *"In the last days . . . I will pour out my Spirit on all people. Your sons and daughters will prophesy, your young men will see visions, your old men will dream dreams"* (Acts 2:17 NIV).

This latter day outpouring was to be characterised by, among other things, young men seeing visions. Young visionaries are not always the most welcome people when introduced into a static situation. Joseph was a young and maybe precocious visionary. His style may have left much to be desired, but his vision was authentic. When he shared it with his brothers it resulted in his being thrown out of the family home. Having endured the pain of rejection, he experienced a process of other God-appointed tests and trials until he arrived at his God-ordained destiny. True to his vision he accomplished God's purpose and blessed not only the world, but also his brothers whom he never ceased to love.

Contemporary visionaries

Some who were freshly filled with the Holy Spirit and began to see visions and dream dreams in the 1960s and '70s had similar experiences. Many were asked to leave their churches and started a journey which would ultimately result in new churches being formed, which are increasingly engaging with the needy world and are enjoying genuine success with thousands in their ranks, a burgeoning younger generation of zealots and a growing world missionary strategy.

Frightened Gideons, wondering where the Lord of miracles had gone, are beginning to be clothed with the Holy Spirit, find fresh courage, deal with their own compromise, gather teams of comrades and take the necessary steps of faith to win great victories.

It takes faith and courage to take a handful of friends to a new town, plant a young church and believe God for growth and blessing. But multiplied numbers are developing the kind of teamwork and commitment necessary to enjoy success and are learning to build from a few dozen to a few hundred while crying out to God that ultimately they will have thousands in their ranks.

Building great churches takes tenacity, endurance and Nehemiah-type leadership. I found fresh inspiration when digging into the book that bears his name and feeling the impact of his life.

Broken-hearted by news of Jerusalem's walls being destroyed and its gates burned, he was galvanised into action and energised by an encounter with God. He became the people's general, a giver of hope whose driven urgency and remorseless energy ensured that the seemingly impossible task was completed. The walls were built, the city stood. God's purpose was accomplished.

These biblical characters rose above the trends of their age and proved that God is well able to revolutionise situations if we take Him seriously and respond obediently to His initiatives.

Each of these men had plenty of reason to throw in the towel. They knew what it was to stand alone before they experienced the dizzy heights of success and popularity. Durability characterised them. These were no comic strip supermen, transformed by fleeting visits to telephone kiosks! They learned the hard way. In an age of instant stardom and press-button success, we need to face up to the challenge of painful preparation, often worked out in secret obedience. Faith must be mixed with patience and fortitude.

Each of these three men experienced the agonies of being misunderstood and misrepresented. They not only had to fulfil their calling and complete their own particular tasks, they also had to withstand the pressures of opposition and keep their attitudes pure and holy, free from self-pity, self-justification or retaliation.

All three were men who had their own personal encounters with God. Each saw devastating situations transformed by God's personal intervention.

Desperate to be relevant

The Church is living through a season where it is becoming increasingly preoccupied with the mood swings of the current culture. Impressed and influenced by what is happening in the wider world, the Church has often been scared to be out of step. Many a pastor has found himself directed towards the modern gods of market research and secular management techniques.

Market research might help us to find out what will make the Church more appealing to people, but the danger is that we will end up with a consumer-driven church. Marketing makes the consumer the final authority, assuming that "the customer is always right". Medical doctors would never function on that basis!

In a desperate endeavour to be relevant, some have adjusted the gospel to make it a message of mere personal fulfilment or meeting felt needs. Others, in an attempt not to offend their contemporaries, adjust and adapt the biblical message to such a degree that they earn the scorn of self-confessed unbelievers such as Matthew Parris who, writing in *The Times*, castigates such Christians for "modifying their morality . . . from a fear of becoming isolated from changing public morals". He continues, "It is time that convinced Christians stopped trying to reconcile their spiritual beliefs with the modern age and understood that if one thing comes clearly through every account we have of Jesus' teaching, it is that His followers are not urged to accommodate themselves to their age, but to the mind of God. Christianity is not supposed to be comfortable or feel 'natural' . . . 'inclusive', 'moderate' or 'sensible'. Christianity is inching its way up a philosophical cul-de-sac. The Church stands for revealed truth and divine inspiration or it stands for nothing."[1]

While some are abandoning their Christian distinctives others are gladly embracing them and discovering their true dynamic. They are enjoying success. Lives are becoming transformed. Churches are being planted. Numbers are growing.

The *Daily Telegraph* recently reported that in the UK more than 1,000 new Christian churches have been created over the last seven years, double the number of Starbucks coffee shops. About 450 branches of Starbucks were opened over the same period.[2] Certainly, churches are also closing, but those that are closing have been largely characterised by the kind of compromise so despised by our critics. Meanwhile, a new era is emerging.

No man can turn the tide. As King Canute discovered, it's beyond human control. But if you watch very carefully it is an observable phenomenon. You can wait attentively and suddenly realise that it has happened. The tide has turned.

When recently gathered with some hundreds of pastors for days of prayer and fasting, it seemed that God impressed upon us that we have entered a new era. It would not be like a new day, when familiar bird sounds and the light of the dawn prepare us for the predictable. It would not be like a new season with its recognisable transitions from heat to cold or from buds to leaves. An era is less recognisable. One man discerns that steam lifts the lid of the kettle and begins to ponder the possibility of steam power. Within a few years steam power has changed the world. Sailing becomes only a sport or hobby. Steam ships encircle the globe and an industrial revolution has broken out. A new era has come.

While it is possible to deplore the closing of many a church building, it is also possible to celebrate the opening of new churches on every side. Warehouses are being purchased, school halls are being hired, even redundant church buildings are being snapped up. The manager of a music shop in London told a friend of mine that he was selling most of his musical instruments to "all these new churches that are starting up around here".

The volume in your hands tells you the story of Bible

characters who lived through the experience of the turning of the tide; real flesh and blood men who battled through against overwhelming odds, the visionary Joseph, the mighty warrior Gideon, and the courageous, enduring builder Nehemiah. I know for myself, as one involved in a movement that has seen 500 churches planted worldwide in the last twenty-five years, that I have been more encouraged and instructed by studying these Bible characters than I have by simply taking on board any recently discovered church growth techniques. It is my conviction that our greatest need is to know God better, to trust Him more implicitly, to obey Him more conscientiously, to take action expecting Him to be true to His promises and thereby bring Him great glory. I pray that as you read through these pages you will recognise our contemporary situation and join in the excitement of catching the turning tide.

Notes

1. Matthew Parris, *The Times*, 9th August, 2003.
2. *Daily Telegraph*, 27th February, 2006.

PART 1

Joseph

"And he sent a man before them —
   Joseph, sold as a slave.
They bruised his feet with shackles,
   his neck was put in irons,
till what he foretold came to pass,
   till the word of the LORD proved him true."
                     (Psalm 105:17–19 NIV)

The Favourite Son

The story of Joseph is unquestionably one of the most beautiful and intriguing stories ever written. It has all the ingredients for great drama: dreams and visions, family feuds involving envy and hatred, passion and lust, scenes of opulence, the squalor of prison and a meteoric rise to power.

Through it all runs the thread of the character central to the entire saga – Joseph – who starts as a naïve boy, displaying a mixture of innocence and arrogance, yet who ends up as a man refined by testing circumstances and exalted to a position of enormous power and prominence.

Who was this man? Where did he come from? As with all family epics, many twists and turns conspired to produce the cradle of circumstances into which he was born, so it is necessary to look behind the scenes a little and to understand something of the family background.

Joseph was an especially loved and longed for child. His father already had ten sons but Rachel, his mother, was childless. Her distress was made more acute as her sister, Leah, who was Jacob's first wife, produced children with apparently effortless ease and regularity. Eventually Rachel's frustration and disappointment drove her to breaking point. She could not cope with passively waiting and hoping any longer. She had to act! She had to do something! The tension created by her unhappiness was destroying her marriage.

One day she was irrationally shouting at Jacob and he was reacting angrily. In desperation she proposed a plan whereby she could become a mother by proxy. If her maid, Bilhah, was to become a surrogate mother, Rachel could take the resulting baby as her own. The plan was put into operation and Dan was born.

Ironically, history was repeating itself. Years before, Jacob's grandfather, Abraham, had found himself in the same plight. His barren wife, Sarah, had offered her maid, Hagar, as a substitute and Ishmael had been born as a result of this. The arrival of this unfortunate child had had disastrous repercussions and yet some two generations later Jacob and Rachel were resorting to the same solution to solve Rachel's childlessness. They had not learned from Abraham's experience that short cutting God's way inevitably leads to complications and confusion even if it provides a short-term quick result.

Rachel exultantly cried out, "God has vindicated me!" when Dan was born, but this was a lie. It was not God's plan and the name Dan, which means "God has vindicated me", eventually disappeared from the record. This can be found in Revelation 7, which records the final list of all the tribes of Israel. Dan's name is not among them, but Joseph's name is there and that of Manassah, his son. (In the end Joseph had a double portion as was foretold.)

God does not need our engineering and manipulating to bring about His purposes. Rachel eventually conceived the longed for child that God had already chosen and planned for, even though she had allowed frustration and disappointment to push her into experimenting with alternatives.

It is by faith and patience that we are to inherit God's blessings. Too often churches have plenty of bright ideas about how they can produce spiritual offspring and it can be hard to wait for God because it can be costly to do things His way. Why be thorough and painstaking when you can get quick results by other means? Why implement scriptural principles of foundation laying and church building when you can import something colourful and appealing that yields quick results? It can be costly and painful getting the foundations right and to build surely and thoroughly, especially when other churches, which seem content with more superficial methods, apparently prosper.

We have to ask some questions: What is our main objective? Self-vindication or a child of God's choosing? Something that grows quickly and fades fast or something that has slow, small beginnings but which will stand strong and secure because it has been initiated by God and nurtured His way?

Let patience have its perfect work among us. God's work, done in God's times and in God's way, will produce God's fruit.

The favourite son

At last Joseph was born. He was special to his father because he was the son of his old age and the son of his beloved wife, Rachel, who had won his heart as a young man. How Jacob lavished his love on Joseph! Perhaps Jacob's joy in Joseph blinded him to the antagonism that such blatant favouritism produced in his ten other sons, because he even favoured him with a significant gift – a coat of many colours. Such a coat was not merely ornamental; it was a sign that the birthright was being passed to Joseph. Reuben should have had this birthright but he had been disqualified for committing sexual sin. All the other brothers were passed over and the birthright given to Joseph, so it is no wonder that jealousy began to take root in their hearts!

Joseph's behaviour added further fuel to the fire of their

envy. With the naïve unwariness of a seventeen-year-old he reported back to his father about some questionable activities that his brothers were indulging in. This so exacerbated their hostility to Joseph that they could hardly bring themselves to speak to him. However, in happy ignorance – or was he just plain obnoxious – he fanned the flame yet again by recounting a dream that he had received.

In his dream Joseph and his brothers were binding sheaves of corn in a field when suddenly Joseph's sheaf arose and all the brothers' sheaves prostrated themselves around it. Understandably the brothers were more inflamed at this dream and even Jacob rebuked Joseph when he recounted a dream in which eleven stars and the sun and the moon were bowing down to him. The boy was obviously getting delusions of grandeur.

Poor Joseph! The visionary, the dreamer, so blessed and excited at being the recipient of such revelation hardly realised what antagonism was being stirred up in the hearts of those who had not been granted such revelation and on one day an unexpected opportunity for revenge arose. Jacob sent Joseph to find his brothers who were tending the flocks way out in the country. The brothers saw him coming and plotted to kill him. However, Reuben managed to restrain them from actual murder and they threw him down a well instead, eventually then selling him to a camel train that was bound for Egypt.

So, the extraordinary drama unfolds, containing as much intrigue, jealousy and hatred as a television soap opera. Yet, it has far more significance and purpose than a mere entertaining tale. It is not only the true account of a man's life, for we find woven into it another story told from God's perspective:

Two generations before God had told Abraham,

"Know for certain that your descendants will be strangers in a land that is not theirs, where they will be enslaved and oppressed

four hundred years . . . afterward they will come out with many possessions . . . in the fourth generation they will return here."

(Genesis 15:13–14, 16)

Joseph was a key part of a plan that was far broader in its scope than one man's life and yet the details of that life were so important to the success of the plan. A sovereign God was unfolding His divine purposes that would reach down the ages and His plan for the nation of Israel hinged upon the life of this young man.

God needed a man who He could trust in a position of enormous power. This man, therefore, had to be utterly impervious to charm and flattery, not given to vindictiveness and had to be free from hidden guilt. He needed to be a man who had proved himself reliable, hard working and efficient, skilled in administration, wise and compassionate.

Where would God find such a paragon? He would select a man before he was born, place him in a certain family environment and put him through a rigorous training programme. Joseph's reactions to the apparently random and cruel events that he suffered, and his demeanour during them, were crucial to the success of the plan as a whole. Behind the scenes God was at work.

Jesus' words, *"What I do now you know not, but afterwards you will understand"* could have been written over Joseph's life many times. Psalm 105:17 says, *"He sent a man before them, Joseph, who was sold as a slave."* The brothers acted out of envy and spite, but the psalmist claims that God was responsible!

Seeing Visions and Dreaming Dreams

The Bible speaks of a God who reigns over everything. Many, like Joseph, know what it is to be tossed about on the waves of life, but this truth can hold them like an anchor. When circumstances change, sometimes suddenly and dramatically, do we still know who is on the throne? God rules over everything and the way He establishes His rule is not through vague patronage from heaven, but by being involved in the detail of individual lives. This is why, just as Joseph's brothers were plotting to eliminate him, a caravan of nameless Ishmaelite merchants happened to arrive. The timing was perfect and God's plan entered the next phase.

We see this same phenomenon happen again and again in the Bible. The story of Esther is a complicated one, but one detail is crucial: one night the king could not sleep. This seemingly trivial event proved to be pivotal to the nation's history and God arranged the king's insomnia in order to bring about His plans. God rules over amazing details of timing!

He also rules over mighty nations – over China, India, Russia and the USA. He is King. He lifts up men and puts them down. He closes China and lets communism rampage through the land. He promotes a common language. He uses communism to deal with the challenge of a rampant idolatry and then opens the door again. The next thing we hear is that throughout China there are millions of Christians.

So Joseph, who seemed to be going from one catastrophe to another, was actually safe in the hands of Almighty God. He had been chosen by God and was being prepared for a part to play in history.

We have also been chosen to participate in good works that have been preordained by God! When this awesome fact grips us we are able to take pressure, delay, opposition or hindrance, because God has laid hold of us and said, "This is My chosen instrument to accomplish My purposes."

We are not just a mass of reactions to circumstances. Philosophers, sociologists and psychologists will explain our lives, personalities and characters from the human perspective. However, if I am assured that God is over all then I am able to see things from a divine viewpoint. I can ask with excitement, "What will God do with my life?" and, as people with destiny we should, like Paul, make it our ambition to lay hold of that which God has predetermined for us.

Visions and dreams

Before continuing with the intriguing story of Joseph I want to draw your attention to something in Joseph's experience that has a familiar New Testament ring to it. Maybe you have noticed a phrase being used that is reminiscent of a quotation from the book of Acts. Now, here was a man who saw visions and dreamed dreams!

Tragically, as Joseph recounted his dreams to his brothers they turned against him and threw him out. Yet, as he submitted to the pressures of God's training programme he became a strong and mature man who ultimately led his brothers into blessing. His visions were vindicated, his family was saved from disaster, and so was the whole of Egypt.

Here, I believe, we have a picture that is similar to what is happening today. God promised in the prophecy of Joel that He would pour His Spirit on all people and that young and old would see visions and dream dreams. Many Christians world-wide have been freshly filled with the Holy Spirit and have started to experience supernatural gifts. Yet often, as they try to share their testimonies, they have not been well received. Maybe this occurs because they have been insensitive in the way they share them or perhaps they have plunged in unwisely and seem to present a threat rather than the promise of abundant life. However it happens it is sadly true that many people have found that sharing these visions has resulted in rejection of both them and their messages.

Sometimes Christians become put out, even offended, when someone whom they may regard as an upstart – maybe even a "younger brother" – claims to have had experiences of the Holy Spirit. They cannot take such people seriously and yet there they are having visions, prophecies and getting altogether too much of the limelight!

It is heartbreaking when Christians respond so negatively to the blessing of another Christian and Joseph's brothers were not the only ones to react this way. When David, young and brave, boldly strode into the Israelite camp one day and offered to meet Goliath's challenge his big brothers were shocked and offended at what they regarded as sheer presumption.

Joseph may have been a green young man, full of himself and irritating in self-assurance, but he was speaking the truth. He *had* seen a vision! Tragically some people, when hearing the testimony of another, read into that testimony an implied comment on themselves:

"So, you see visions, do you?"

"So, you've received the Holy Spirit and speak in tongues, do you?"

"So, you're saying that you have something that I don't have, are you?"

"You're making out that you're better than I am, are you?"

"You're implying that I'm some sort of second-class Christian?"

Tragically, people leap to conclusions and get defensive, hostile and bitter.

One Christian wrote a book in which he sarcastically described Christians in charismatic churches as "the charismatic super-sainthood movement". Tension is brought to God's family as Christians react against each other and it can become very difficult to share testimony honestly without being misunderstood.

There is a wonderful story told in the Old Testament about four lepers outside the city of Samaria which was in the throes of a siege. The enemy had unaccountably fled and they discovered tent after tent full of food, clothes and riches! Jubilantly they exclaimed, "This is not a day to keep silent! Let's go and tell the city!" They were only lepers, but they had stumbled onto something that had to be shared!

They returned to the city and the initial response to their news was one of suspicion, although eventually the king was persuaded to send out a search party to investigate. The lepers' story was confirmed and the starving Samaritans rushed out to plunder the camp.

There are many Christians today who feel starved. They are despondent and besieged by hosts of enemy doubts and fears. Then comes news of abundance! The miracle working God does not belong to some past privilege! He is at work now and wants to bless us too! The messengers may be less than perfect – even a bit uncouth – but the message is genuine.

The food is there and the only barriers are cynicism and unbelief.

When Joseph shared his testimony he was rejected. The temptation to keep quiet about received blessings can be immense as no one enjoys rejection. But truth and honesty were, and are, at stake. Did Joseph have a genuine vision or not?

Some people today, like Joseph, are being prepared for future ministry and as time goes on foundational ministries such as apostles and prophets will emerge. Will there be enthusiastic and happy responses? Maybe from some, but from others, inevitably, there will be cynical remarks and rumours.

"Have you heard? So-and-so claims to be an apostle."

"Really? Thinks he can rival St Paul, does he?"

"Worse! Probably claims infallibility!"

"Well, we can't possibly go along with that heretical nonsense!"

"Of course, God exalts the humble. He can't possibly bless such presumption. It can't be of God."

As men honestly seek to rediscover the teaching of the New Testament and the place of the ministries listed in Ephesians 4, there will be a strong temptation to dilute our terminology with more palatable words. We could say that someone "gives counsel" into a church or is "helping it to develop". In an attempt to make it more acceptable we could talk about people having something of an "apostolic function" rather than call them apostles outright. However, if we do lose our edge we shall lose our vision and then finally lose our way. We must be honest and true to our vision even though we may have to pay the same price that Joseph paid in terms of rejection.

It is the responsibility of those who see visions and dream dreams to be true to these visions. They must also continually seek God's help to put no unnecessary stumbling block before their brothers through unwarranted arrogance. May God help us all as we seek to go forward to fulfil His purpose in our generation.

A Successful Man

Joseph could have protested, "I was only true to my vision. I only shared what God had shown me! Now look at me – separated from my parents, my brothers, far from home in another country, a slave with no rights and no future. It's all so unfair!" He could have been devastated by these experiences but, amazingly, we read that in Egypt Joseph *became a successful man*. Although his circumstances were grim he prospered because God was with him.

What does this tell me about Joseph? Firstly, it tells me that he refused to live in the past. He flatly rejected the temptation to harbour resentment for what his brothers had done to him and he was not wallowing in self-pity. However, many people have their whole lives spoilt because they carry hurts and grudges about past events. They remember the way that someone spoke to them, the way they were treated, sometimes from years ago. Many people nurse an ugly root of bitterness and then wonder why their lives bear little fruit. They long to pray, be filled with the Spirit and be fed by the Bible, but inwardly they smoulder with a bitterness that spoils the work of grace in their lives.

I wonder if you are ever tempted to mutter to yourself, "If only that had not happened all would have been well . . . If only they hadn't treated me like that I would be on course ... It's not my fault that I'm not making any progress..." We often make excuses for ourselves while bitterness festers within and distorts our growth. Many ask, "Lord, why did you let this happen to me?" We want God to explain everything to us, yet biblical characters often went through all kinds of pressures that were left unexplained. They had to learn to leave things with God.

You might be smarting from unexpected heartaches, broken engagements, illnesses, bereavement or loss and any of these could give rise to bitterness. Perhaps you are resentful towards someone or a group of people who have distorted your testimony. Maybe receiving the baptism of the Holy Spirit was one of the happiest moments of your life but then went on to lead to angry accusations against you which escalated into a furious row and ended with you being asked to leave. You may be seething with bitterness at what you regard as cruel and unjust treatment, but you must determine to leave the past behind and walk away free.

If you carry in your spirit things against God or against your brothers and sisters, you will never experience all that God has for you however much you apply yourself to other things such as prayer, Bible reading or trying to become free in worship. You will never be recorded as a "successful man" or a "prosperous woman" because the root of bitterness will spoil everything. Joseph had many reasons to be sour, yet he rejected them.

Forgive and forget

We must break free using a deliberate decision! As children of God we deliberately decide to forgive because God has given us grace to do so. God has shown mercy to us sinners and thereby provided us with powerful motivation for forgiving others. To encourage us Jesus spoke some awesome words:

> *"For if you forgive others for their transgressions, your heavenly Father will also forgive you. But if you do not forgive others, then your Father will not forgive your transgressions."*
> (Matthew 6:14–15)

Jesus taught us a prayer that contains these lines: *"Forgive us our trespasses as we forgive those who trespass against us."* In other words we are saying, "Forgive me Lord in the way that I forgive others." If we are not giving away forgiveness we are not going to receive any ourselves. Will you maintain the discipline of praying that prayer regularly? Can you ask for forgiveness, secure in knowing you will receive it because you have a forgiving spirit yourself?

Decide to live like this! You can do it. Do not say, "I'm only human." You are not only human; you are one who has found grace in the eyes of the Lord. You have been forgiven much! Jesus taught quite clearly and plainly that for a believer to cling to resentment towards someone is an outrage before him. He told a parable about a man who was forgiven a vast debt and who then demanded the repayment of a very small amount owing to him. When this man's refusal to forgive was discovered by the one who had released him from his great debt there was outrage! How could he insist on repayment for such a petty claim when he had been let off so much himself?

Jesus made it very plain that we do not need some special touch from God to be set free to forgive. We do not need to seek prayer from a preacher or special ministry. We forgive because we are children of God and the Spirit of Christ is in us. If there is one thing that Christians should excel at it is forgiving other people.

Walk by faith

Not only did Joseph forgive and forget the past, he also steadfastly maintained a stance of faith. His testimony is one of the outstanding illustrations that God makes all things work together for good to those who love Him and are called according to His purpose. Living long before Romans 8:28 was penned, Joseph seemed to have the truth written on his heart. It is one of the great promises that should make Christians shine in a world where people are tormented by fear and anxiety. When we are assured of God's overruling providence we can live with poise and praise. The fact that everything is working together for good becomes a well of water springing up in our spirit. Having confidence that God is on the throne is what changes and transforms us. Having forgiven and forgotten we maintain our joy and peace by believing God and in this way we become lights in the world.

In Philippians Paul tells us as Christians to,

> *"Do all things without grumbling or disputing; so that you will prove yourselves to be blameless and innocent, children of God above reproach in the midst of a crooked and per- verse generation, among whom you appear as lights in the world..."*
>
> (Philippians 2:14–15)

Often we wonder how to shine as a light in the world and here is one way that is very clear. We are in the midst of a world that complains all the time. Sadly, the world seems to complain about any situation. If it has been a fine week for weather we often hear the complaint that it is bound to rain because the weekend is coming! People complain about the buses and trains being late, about the way the office is run, about the management, about people. We constantly hear this dull, grating noise of complaint and ingratitude.

The Church shines as a light in the world, not only by proclaiming Jesus in the streets but by also doing all things without grumbling and complaining. This is enough to make you shine today! Remember to keep shining! Encourage one another all the time – husbands, wives and parents. We must stop one another in our tracks and say, "Remember you're a Christian! Remember to do all things without grumbling or complaining!"

This proves that we are "children of God without fault". Joseph was like this and it made him stand out. He had learned to give thanks in everything and not complain.

There are two languages in the world: the language of complaint and the language of thanksgiving, and there are some who live in between and can speak both. Don't live on the border learning a foreign language – be a true native of Zion!

Beware the dim, distant future

Joseph was not dwelling in the past, but neither was he living in the future in a haze of dreams and fantasies. The fact that Joseph was a successful man is clear proof that he was not projecting everything into the future. How easily he could have been dominated by the thought, "One day I'll get out of here."

If we project everything into the future we can fail to apply God's grace in the present so we are forever living in frustration and dissatisfaction. It is so easy to live in a world of unreality: "When I get away from home and leave my unbelieving family I can mix with other Christians and be a real living testimony." Later on at university we can argue, "I must get my degree first. When I've finished at university I'll really live for God." Then, having met Mr or Miss Right we think that once we are married and have our own Christian home we will shine for God.

So often we chafe at the restrictions of the moment and use them as an excuse for not bearing fruit. We can dream that sometime in the future God will begin to move mightily by His Spirit and we shall do great exploits, but everything is in the distant, misty future in a life supposedly free from present complications and limitations. Some argue that they know they have received a call and when they become full-time it will change everything. Yet Joseph bore fruit while he was in the house of his master, the Egyptian. In spite of all the restrictions Joseph was a successful man and the Lord even blessed Potiphar's house because of him. Eventually Potiphar gave him more responsibility so that the Lord blessed all that he owned on account of Joseph.

Kingdom principles

In the book of Luke Jesus laid down some definite kingdom principles:

> *"He who is faithful in a very little thing is faithful also in much; and he who is unrighteous in a very little thing is unrighteous also in much. Therefore if you have not been faithful in the use of unrighteous wealth, who will entrust the true riches to you? And if you have not been faithful in the use of that which is another's, who will give you that which is your own?"*

> (Luke 16:10–12)

Here we see three statements that Jesus gave as laws of the kingdom which must affect our way of life. We have to be faithful in the little things. Joseph was not found muttering, "I suppose I'd better serve in this awful place. One day when I get out they'll see what I'm made of. One day they're going to bow to me – one day – meanwhile I have to look after this God-forsaken hole that is not worthy of me!"

Do we find Joseph murmuring this resentment? No. He brought blessing to his master's house! As we tackle our present responsibilities faithfully God takes note!

God is looking for those who are faithful in the use of "worldly wealth" such as money, possessions and houses – in fact, everyday commodities that are part of day-to-day life. We can make false distinctions between what is "of the world" and what is "of the kingdom" and all those things we think are not of the kingdom we relegate to the secular and regard as worldly. The next step is to say, "These things do not pertain to the kingdom so it does not matter how I treat them." The temptation quickly follows to be less than thorough at work, to rush off quickly to attend meetings leaving things undone, or to be inefficient in the name of "putting first the kingdom of God". God, however, is looking for diligence and righteousness while we are dealing with this "worldly wealth".

Joseph's experience in Potiphar's house was all part of his training for the ministry that lay ahead of him. God is now looking on many a life and asking, "Does this one qualify to have authority in my Church? Can he or she cope with the full glare of publicity? Can his life stand up to scrutiny? Has he already proved himself honourable in small details when no one is watching but me?"

Are you faithful at work? Do you do a good job or do you think, "I can't wait to get away from this awful place." God forewarns us, "And if you have not been trustworthy with someone else's property, who will give you property of your own?" David looked after a few sheep that were his father's, not his, yet he did it so meticulously, so carefully and so responsibly that God lifted him from shepherding a few sheep and said, "Now you shepherd my nation!"

Joseph was faithful though just a slave in a foreign land. As we rejoice in the discovery of spiritual gifts and charismatic worship we are not to fool ourselves that God is no longer interested in character development. He monitors our reactions to see whether we are ready for true riches, whether we can have what is our own.

For example, I am sure that He watches over the way we have cared for our small house group. God would say, "I have watched over the way you have cared for your little flock and not deplored the fact that you are not speaking to hundreds. I have watched your faithfulness." God watches us just as He watched over Joseph.

So, Joseph was not preoccupied with looking back and neither was he only dreaming of the future. He was living in the present and using it as a training programme. He was running the race and running it well when suddenly, into his world, came another fearful challenge.

"Lie with Me"

We do not live in a spiritually neutral environment. We live in a world where Satan has many ways of attacking and undermining. He can assume many different disguises to trick us and discredit the work of God. As we follow the story of Joseph, which is so relevant to the days in which we live, we see Potiphar's wife appear on the scene. Here was Joseph, away from home and its restrictions, young and handsome and beginning to make his mark and Potiphar's wife began to turn her eyes on him. Her husband was often away from home and she was alone, available and willing. Powerful temptation suddenly stared Joseph in the face.

This woman who had power and authority found Joseph desirable and wanted him for herself. The challenge was sudden and outrageous. Suddenly, and quite openly, she invited him to lie with her and this young man found himself encountering a situation that he had never faced before. Without warning an unexpected road to fulfilment opened before him, alluring, fascinating and begging to be explored. Temptation is often like this – sudden and with the promise of instant satisfaction. This is why it is so powerful. "I can satisfy you now, immediately," it whispers so urgently. But it can ruin a whole life in a moment of time.

Earlier in the Old Testament we find Esau stumbling from the fields, famished. He smelled the inviting aroma of meat, which Jacob was cooking, and blurted out, "Give me some of that red stew" (see Genesis 25:30). His flesh was crying out for fulfilment, its demand overriding his spirit: "I want to be satisfied and I want it now!" This expression of Esau's so sums up the longings of the flesh. When Jacob replied that it would cost him his inheritance Esau answered that he cared nothing for his inheritance.

"Give me some of that red stew now!" Temptation has the ability to make all that is spiritual and godly fade from view while the flesh clamours for immediate satisfaction. For Esau, a massive tug-of-war began as this young man was invited to forfeit his inheritance and indulge his appetite. He failed miserably.

Young people today leave home, go away to college, to university, or even just on holiday, where they find that temptations they have never faced before are suddenly upon them with ferocious intensity. It is all so easy now; it is all so possible. The restrictions have disappeared and temptation can suddenly be overwhelming.

For Joseph not only was it sudden, it was also sustained. Genesis tells us that she entreated him *"day after day"* (Genesis 39:10). Day after day! It's a wonder how Joseph maintained his purity. He was not like Samson who withstood at first but when pressed day after day gave in. Sometimes, just like this, we face prolonged periods of temptation.

Not only was it sustained though – it was subtle as well. Genesis continues, *"He refused to go to bed with her..."* However, there was maybe an alternative – he would not actually go to bed with her but he could maybe spend some time with her, perhaps indulging in a little harmless flirtation, seeing just how far they could go.

People often think that they can play with fire and remain unburned. They do not intend to be totally, irrevocably committed to adultery, but they cannot bring themselves to be drastic and final either. They indulge in a little intrigue, but before they retreat the flirtation has been fanned into a fire. This subtle alternative confronted Joseph.

After this Satan played another ace. Joseph knew that Potiphar's wife had authority through her husband. Joseph may have thought, "Perhaps she could get me out of this situation – if I went along with her she could maybe pull some strings to get me out of this whole predicament..." Surely Satan understood Joseph's awful sense of being unloved, lonely and away from home. Other people did not love him but now, suddenly, this woman desired him. She was showing him attention when no one else was. The powerful subtlety of it all! Satan whispered insidious arguments, relentlessly pressurising Joseph to throw away his purity.

No one can see

Not only was this attack sudden, sustained and subtle, it was also secret. Potiphar's wife said, "There's no one else here. No one else will know about it – just you and me. No one needs to know; no one can see what is happening here in the dark between us..."

The truth of the matter is that all of heaven was looking on. All of heaven was watching this young man, who was called by God, in the midst of great pressures and difficulties. He was in the centre of God's will, set for a glorious future fulfilling the purpose of God. Today we might think that there is no one looking at us but in fact, all of heaven is looking on and wondering, "Will this young man or woman triumph or will they throw everything away in one moment of foolishness?"

So often the devil tells us lies such as, "No one can see." We forget that God is with us all the time and we cannot hide from Him. Everything is open to Him and He observes our response on the evil day. It is no good saying, "My New Year's resolution is that I will not be tempted this year" because there will *always* be temptation. Even Jesus was tempted! In Deuteronomy 8:2 it says, *"God has led you in the wilderness these forty years . . . to know what was in your heart."* He allows us to be in situations that reveal our inner motivations. His aim is to make us like Jesus, who loved righteousness and hated iniquity.

How did Joseph overcome? First of all he overcame by being the very opposite to Eve in the garden. God had said to Eve, "You may eat of any of the trees except one," but because she had already become preoccupied with that other tree when the devil approached her, she was open to temptation.

Joseph's attitude was completely different. When Potiphar's wife spoke to him he replied, "I thank God that He has given me everything else. It is only right that He should withhold you." I believe that his reply was rooted in the attitude we noted earlier, namely that he received all things without grumbling or complaining. He was enjoying all that God had already given and he had a positive attitude and a clear perspective to his life.

If our whole attitude to life is essentially one of thanksgiving, praise and acceptance of all that God has given, when some other thing is offered to us we are already fulfilled after having already accepted from God what He has graciously given. This is to be our basic attitude to life. People who are bitter, who feel that things are not all they should be, who complain that "nobody loves me", are far more vulnerable to this kind of temptation because they are always longing for something different in which to find fulfilment.

Call a spade a spade

Joseph had another weapon he could use to overcome temptation: he did not hesitate to name what Potiphar's wife offered
as "evil". He replied, "Why should I do this great evil?" He was
under no illusions about that.

We must also start calling a spade a spade. The world tries to
deceive us by cunningly changing the terminology. It uses
many euphemisms for sin, preferring to call it "indiscretion".
The terminology has changed so that sin has become acceptable and is no longer regarded as sin if it is "meaningful". Sexual
experimentation is OK as long as people "love" each other – we
hear this so often. "We love each other, don't we? That's all
that matters . . ."

Across our nation there are a vast number of young people
who see visions and dream dreams – young people, even
children, who are entering into a new spiritual dimension and
who are living in the midst of a crooked and perverse
generation, a generation that says, "Come, lie with us."
Promiscuity is the accepted thing: "Everyone else is doing it,
so why should you be the only girl in the class who is a virgin?"
Siren voices beckon, "Come lie with us, come and be like us."

Joseph overcame by being very clear about the issues. We
have to be equally as clear and say, "To do such-and-such is a
great evil." It is not just "free love"; it is not just "meaningful";
it is a great evil!

We need to wake up to the fact that compromise abounds in
all areas of life, not just in sexual sin. The stealing that takes
place at work, the shoplifting, the tax fiddles – they are all
regarded as commonplace and are increasingly acceptable.
There are major companies that build a percentage into their
accounts to compensate for the amount that will be stolen from
them by their employees – taken away from the factory in

pockets, in the boots of cars and on the backs of lorries. It is a way of life.

In sport we find the "professional foul", which is really just cheating, and it spoils and robs us of the joys of true sport. The moral fibre of our nation is being whittled away as the world invites us to, "Come, lie with us." Why do you have to be so different? Because behind it all is the devil with his antagonism and all his passion to spoil. Joseph called it a great evil. He called it what it was and saw that it was against God: "Why should I do this great evil and sin against God?" A generation that is losing all its signposts is a nation that has forgotten that sin is an offence against God.

"Sin" is a biblical word with wide-ranging implications. It is not just that I sin against my brother or my sister and so spoil their lives, but my sin is also against God. In the end this was what devastated David after he had sinned with Bathesheba. He admitted, *"Against you, you only, have I sinned"* (Psalm 51:4 NIV). He could not escape his crippling guilt.

Joseph, however, was steadfast. Day by day he refused to give in and maintained his integrity. He could not tell his master and because he was a slave he could not run away. He was shut in. What was he to do?

Finally Potiphar's wife forced herself on him. As she clung to his sleeve willing him to share her life he wrenched himself free and fled leaving her holding his garment, so desperate was he to leave the danger zone. All heaven must have rejoiced. He had come through the test! He was vindicated!

In the film *Chariots of Fire* about two young men who were invited to Paris to race in the 1924 Olympic Games, one of them, a Christian called Eric Liddell, was horrified to find that the heat for the one hundred-yard race would be run on a Sunday. Large pressure was put on him by the authorities, but his sustained refusal to run on the Sunday brought the film to a thrilling climax: he finally agreed to run in the four hundred-yard race, a distance for which he had not trained. As he was waiting, ready to run the race of a lifetime, someone thrust a scrap of paper into his hand on which was written, "Those who honour God, God will honour." The starting pistol broke the silence and the race was underway. The excitement mounted as this tremendous sprinter thundered round the track clutching the crumpled promise in his hand. And of course, he won a famous victory! A friend of mine who saw the film in London when it first came out told me that at the end the entire cinema audience stood up and applauded.

Liddell was lifted shoulder high and carried out triumphant in his victory. He had won the race; he had been true to his convictions and was gloriously vindicated. But back to Joseph – he was also true to his convictions and look what happened to him: his coat was torn from his back and Potiphar's wife screamed that he had molested her. Her lies were believed and he was thrown into prison. And yet God still had a great redemptive purpose for Joseph.

Promotion to Prison

Full of integrity and resisting sin at great cost, Joseph was not carried shoulder high by an exultant crowd, but was instead lied against, ridiculed and thrown into prison. Honouring God does not always result in being acclaimed by the crowd. Joseph's integrity cost him everything. However, if we could see this disaster from heaven's perspective we would see angels rejoicing over Joseph, even as men were casting him into prison. From God's viewpoint Joseph had triumphed. He was on course and ready for the next stage that would prepare him for God's ultimate purpose in his life.

God carefully, painstakingly, orchestrates the details of our lives. Salvation is free but preparation for spiritual authority is often costly and difficult.

Joseph was in the furnace being prepared for future ministry. Psalm 105:19 reminds us that the word of the Lord *refined* him. Elijah knew a similar experience to this: this amazing man had hardly arrived on the scene when God directed him to the brook at Cherith to be fed by ravens. Day by hot, dusty day the meagre trickle dwindled in the drought. Elijah must have watched this anxiously. At last God stepped in: "Elijah, go to Zarephath where I have commanded a widow woman to feed you." However, one thing God did not mention was that the widow woman was starving and nearly at death's door! Having arrived at this hopeless rendezvous, Elijah discovered all kinds of tests awaiting him. While he was there her only son was going to die. (The very name "Zarephath" means "the place of refining, the place of the crucible".)

God tries His saints. He puts them into the crucible to refine their lives. When we tell God that we want to serve Him with our lives in order to see His kingdom come, He tests us to see if this is what we really want. Often this test involves going through a furnace and we are usually tempted to ask, "Lord, how much longer is this pressure going to last? I can't understand why it is so prolonged and so difficult."

Why did Elijah have to go from one pressure to another? Because God had a great plan for him. He was going to stand before the whole nation of Israel and call down fire from heaven, and then open the skies after three years of drought. God painstakingly prepares a man who is going to have a significant ministry.

Sure foundations

Let me put it another way: why are foundations laid under a building? I recall how some years ago we endured a terrible furnace experience in our church. God spoke to us in prophecy: "I know how large the building will be. That is why I am taking such pains over the foundations." God knows what He wants to build and how significant our testimony is going to be, and so He takes time with us. When you question why life is so difficult God replies, *"You do not realise now what I am doing, but later you will understand"* (John 13:7 NIV).

We must take courage from the Scriptures. When encouraged by them we can see how the story ends. However, God's Word must work its way into our hearts. Psalm 66 says,

"For You have tried us, O God;
You have refined us as silver is refined.
You brought us into the net;
You laid an oppressive burden upon our loins.
You made men ride over our heads;
We went through fire and through water,
Yet You brought us out into a place of abundance."

(Psalm 66:10–12)

You can write the word "Joseph" against this in your Bible because this is exactly what he went through until he was eventually brought out to *"a place of a abundance."*

So often when we go through pressure we wonder if the devil is oppressing us, but even when evil men seem responsible they only prove to be God's instruments in a great plan.

Paul says,

"For we do not want you to be unaware, brethren, of our affliction which came to us in Asia, that we were burdened excessively, beyond our strength, so that we despaired even of life; indeed, we had the sentence of death within ourselves so that we would not trust in ourselves, but in God who raises the dead."

(2 Corinthians 1:8–9)

He continues,

"But we have this treasure in earthen vessels, so that the surpassing greatness of the power will be of God and not from ourselves; we are afflicted in every way, but not crushed; perplexed, but not despairing; persecuted, but not forsaken; struck down, but not destroyed; always carrying about in the body the dying of Jesus, so that the life of Jesus also may be manifested in our body. For we who live are constantly being

delivered over to death for Jesus' sake, so that the life of Jesus also may be manifested in our mortal flesh."

(2 Corinthians 4:7–11)

What does a furnace do? It burns up rubbish, which is not only dirty but also unnecessary and irrelevant; things that are not worth clinging to; things that take up space and clutter our lives. God wants to remove the litter from our lives. He wants us to see what is essential and what has lasting value. We are running a race and we cannot run well if we are hampered by excess baggage.

Burning the rubbish

In the parable of the sower Jesus said that there are those who immediately respond to the word, then the sun rises. Their swift response is tested. Jesus did not say, "And then, one day, the sun *might* rise." The sun has a definite tendency to rise! Our impulsive and often emotional responses are tested.

God not only burns up our emotional responses, He also challenges our cold, doctrinal correctness when it is not built on genuine faith! We can be meticulous in defending such doctrines as the sovereignty of God and yet be tense, nervous and defensive because these doctrines have never entered out hearts. No, if we believe these great doctrines they should build security into our lives – total peace and rest. Those who believe in the sovereignty of God should be like a rock, secure and immovable, not frightened men and women instead.

It is better that we find out what we really are through the fire. It delivers us from our own self-sufficiency, from thinking we can make it on our own. When we go through the test, we discover how weak and needy we are and realise the danger of being exalted prematurely to a position that we cannot handle.

God is preparing His Church for end-time prominence when she shall arise and shine, and nations will turn to her light and kings to the brightness of her rising. Then the mountain of the house of the Lord will rise above all other mountains and all the nations will flow to it. What an exalted position His Church shall have! God wants every precious stone tried, tested, safe, secure and able to handle the glory as well as the pressure.

So, the Church will be full of genuinely meek people who know that when left to themselves they are weak and helpless. Jesus, our meek and lowly King, is calling an army of believers who have no confidence in the flesh.

When we go through pressure we often feel "storm-tossed, afflicted and not comforted" and some even question their salvation. We can miss God's purpose if we are not careful. There are three wrong ways in which to respond:

1. It says in Hebrews 12:5, *"My son, **do not regard lightly** the discipline of the Lord"* (emphasis added). Do not shrug it off and fail to respond to God's dealings with you.

2. It then says, *"[Don't] **faint** when you are reproved by him"* (emphasis added), as some children do when you correct them. They think that you are always against them and collapse in self-pity.

3. The writer of Hebrews warns us to make sure *"that **no bitter root** grows up to cause trouble and defile many"* (Hebrews 12:15 NIV, emphasis added).

God is training us and pressure is of benefit to those who are trained by it!

A fruitful vine by a spring

How did Joseph survive? What made him succeed through the whole experience? Genesis 49:22 describes Joseph as a fruitful vine by a spring, whose branches went over the wall. What a beautiful testimony! It's also very reminiscent of Jeremiah 17:7−8:

> *Blessed is the man who trusts in the* LORD
> *And whose trust is the* LORD.
> *For he will be like a tree planted by the water,*
> *That extends its roots by a stream*
> *And will not fear when the heat comes;*
> *But its leaves will be green,*
> *And it will not be anxious in a year of drought*
> *Nor cease to yield fruit.''*

The tree that sends its roots down into the stream does not fear when the heat comes. Though Joseph was in furnace conditions, his roots were in the stream – he was still trusting God. Not only did he continue to bear fruit but his bough also climbed up over the wall. He not only kept himself but he also blessed those around him, whether it was Potiphar's household or his fellow prisoners. In spite of his own needs he noticed when the baker and the butler were distressed and asked, "Why is your countenance down? Why do you look so sad?" He still had something to give away and he had grace for himself and for others.

Unwavering faith

In addition to this Joseph retained his confidence in God and childlike faith in the promise of his original visions. How do I know that he kept believing? Because of his response to the baker and the butler when they told Joseph about their dreams. How easily he could have replied, "I used to have dreams! If I were you I would forget it! I had dreams, but I've grown up now!" But he didn't say this. He immediately replied, "Tell me your dreams; I will tell you the interpretation!" There was no cynicism, no disillusionment – Joseph was still believing. Since he had had his dreams everything had gone wrong, but he never excluded God; he still believed! If he was willing to interpret for others he must still have had confidence in his own dream. He did not hesitate and spoke out with confident faith instead of with bitter frustration and disappointment.

The psalmist said, *"I believed, therefore have I spoken"* (Psalm 116:10 AV). Perhaps you have been going through a test and the promise you were given seems so far in the past. Everything has gone wrong. Have you discarded the word that gripped and thrilled you, or are you, like Joseph, still as confident in the word that God gave you when you first heard it?

God wants us to speak because we believe. The heat is not to destroy our faith but to refine it. May God deliver us from throwing away our confidence.

We must be followers of those who, through faith and patience, inherited the promises and we must let God's furnace refine and prepare us for the ministry that He has for us in the future. Psalm 105 tells us that the word of the Lord tested Joseph until the word came to pass. It was certain that the promise of God would "come to pass". Joseph had endured the test and was about to step into the fulfilment of God's promises. He was tested, tried and found to be faithful.

From Prison to Palace

The time eventually came for Joseph's release and the fulfilment of his early vision. He was at last liberated from those confining, restricting walls to emerge centre stage in the world's limelight. But what actually caused his release?

First of all, *God promised* that it would happen. The story started with a definite promise from God, who revealed His purpose by giving the young Joseph two visions. (God has also declared that He will glorify His Son through His Church so this will happen too!)

Secondly, it was because of *Joseph's persevering faithfulness.* Joseph could have disqualified himself time and again but he remained resolute. In absolute integrity he passed from test to test and was changed from one degree of glory to another. God wants us to mature like this. As you are poured from one vessel to another don't complain, but instead believe that God makes all things work together for good!

Thirdly, Joseph emerged because of *his life in the Spirit.* He was still living in his spiritual anointing, using the gifts that God had given him and he still interpreted dreams. Because he did not waste this marvellous gift from God, God unlocked doors for him.

The butler suddenly remembered a man whom he met in prison who lived in a different dimension – not shut into this world's ignorance and barrenness. The supernatural gifts will also provide the breakthrough for the Church in these end times. We are already seeing people who had previously been closed to the gospel opening their hearts as a result of such spiritual gifts as words of knowledge and healings. Sinners seem more impressed by the supernatural than they are with things done pleasantly, decently or with great aesthetic beauty and skill. No one can deny that the Church looks stunningly impressive on such occasions as royal weddings, but the sobering truth is that few are beating on the doors of the church afterward saying, "It was so impressive that you must show us how we can know God like that!"

Beautifully organised occasions are not the answer to life's needs. No, we need the anointing of God to open up the way. Pharaoh recognised it and said that Joseph was a man in whom there was a divine Spirit. This was Joseph's hallmark and it must become the mark of the Church – people in whom there is the divine Spirit!

Joseph was a mature young man, aged thirty years by now, and no longer the abrasive seventeen year old he once was. Likewise, God is going to mature His Church to the fullness of the stature of Christ. Corporately, the Church must step upon the stage as a people in whom the divine Spirit dwells.

Not me, but God

Joseph came out of his furnace in intimate communion with God. The Egyptians challenged him: "We understand that you can interpret dreams" and at once he replied, "It is not in me, but God will." They therefore immediately encountered God and not just a man.

God forbid that we should go into the furnace if we do not come out knowing God better. Paul said that our pressures are to teach us not to trust in ourselves, but in God who raises the dead (see 2 Corinthians 1:9). We lose our *self*-confidence as the furnace shows us what rubbish we are and we discover what God has known about us from the beginning.

Being a young man Joseph could have thought, as many pagans of his day did, that there was a god of the mountains and a god of the valleys, a god of Egypt and a god of Canaan. Facing the challenge of Egypt, he could have regarded his "family religion" as totally inadequate in different circumstances.

Many young people become vulnerable when wondering if their parents' faith will be adequate to face the challenges of modern life, yet Joseph did not surface with such second-hand faith. He boldly declared, "My God will intervene. He rules over everything and has determined these events." So, the mighty Pharaoh met with the Almighty God!

Joseph had a clear understanding that his father's God, his God, was King of the nations. Sometimes it is easier to become apologetic rather than defensive about your beliefs when faced by those who do not believe in God. Joseph, however, did not. He believed that his God was as much a Master of mighty Egypt as He was of lowly Canaan. Wherever Joseph was, be it Potiphar's house or prison, or even before mighty Pharaoh, he was confident in God. Our generation waits to see people who know God in the same way; who do not confront with personal opinions, but speak boldly about their Christian faith in God.

We often hear people complaining that they don't know what is happening to this nation and too often we quickly agree that the nation is in a terrible condition. By God's grace and by His Spirit being in us we need to explain that the nation has turned its back on God and that this is the reason why it has lost its way. We must confront our atheistic nation with God in whom we believe.

Famine conditions

Joseph immediately brought the presence of God into the centre of Pharaoh's predicament. He had dreamed of seven prosperous years followed by seven years of famine. Psalm 105:16 makes an extraordinary statement: "[God] *called for a famine upon the land.*" We once again see God's awe-inspiring providence. The story started when God caused some Ishmaelites to be moving south to Egypt on the very day that the brothers turned against Joseph. God called for the Ishmaelites and here God calls for a famine. Just as we might call a dog God can summon a famine! He rules over all!

Today, a terrible moral famine is stalking our land. The nation is morally bankrupt. There is a famine in the arts – much of our music, theatre and painting seem to reflect emptiness and pessimism.

A very close friend of mine studied at Brighton College of Art. Having completed his degree course he gave me the dubious pleasure of looking at the work of his fellow students. As I walked around the art college I came to the conclusion that there really is a famine in the land! To think that what I saw was the product of years of training! The very atmosphere of the college and my encounters with the students only strengthened my verdict. The dreary depressing work filling the rooms and hanging on the walls was how the young minds had expressed their "famine" on paper and canvas.

There is a famine of fresh ideas, a famine of skill, a famine of steadfastness, a famine of integrity and – the greatest famine of all – a famine of the teaching of God's Word. The worst thing that can ever happen to a nation is for God not to speak any more. In Romans 1 we read a terrible phrase, which occurs three times: *"God gave them up"* (NKJV). When people have refused, rejected and turned their backs, sometimes God gives them up!

Hell is a place where God will never speak again!

There is a dearth of the Word of God being faithfully and powerfully proclaimed in our land and it is leading to moral decadence right across the nation. In Joseph's day God called for famine and what used to be healthy and strong was destroyed – the nation's resources were plundered. And yet wonderfully, on this occasion, the famine was to provide the awful backcloth to the picture of mercy and grace which God was about to paint on it. He created the famine to highlight the resources that Joseph would provide.

We must pray that as darkness covers the earth God will cause the light of the Church to arise in amazing contrast. If we will clearly focus on God and His wonderful promises of grace and mercy we need not panic at the famine, but believe in the Almighty God who overrules all history. It was in this context that Joseph was prepared: His God-given wisdom would revolutionise the situation.

CHAPTER 8

Food for All

Joseph could simply have been delivered from prison and this could have been the end of the story, but instead his deliverance from prison prepared the way for the deliverance of a nation from famine! Joseph stood in the centre of Pharaoh's court and prophesied that prosperity would be followed by famine. In a few years the country would be hit by disaster and he held the key – not only to Egypt's survival, but to that of the surrounding nations as well!

Joseph arrived with all the answers to the needs of his generation and God plans the same for His Church today: He has invested in the Church all that is required. The principles of the kingdom of God provide the answers to all the nation's needs. He is teaching us wonderful principles, which the man in the street has never heard, never grasped, never seen and never thought possible. He has taught us about integrity, family life and the essential covenant of love between husband and wife. He has taught us that security and peace are the results of a marriage where a wife honours and recognises her husband's headship and where the husband unselfishly loves and honours his wife.

Another life-changing principle that God is teaching us is that children who are undisciplined are unloved. If we love our children we will patiently teach them how to behave and how to respect others. We will teach them principles and morality based on God's Word; we will not let them run wild and unrestrained so that they become obnoxious to society, selfish and lawless, unable to make relationships or have any self-respect, security or sense of dignity.

Years ago when one of our sons had a party to celebrate his birthday he invited along half a dozen boys and we organised some games. After a fairly energetic afternoon the parents came to fetch their children and we told one mother how we had been playing games with the boys. She was plainly surprised saying, "But they don't like that sort of thing these days. When we have a party we say, 'Do what you like' and then just hold on for a couple of hours until it's all over!"

But the boys did enjoy organised games. This surprised the mother, firstly because we had taken the time and trouble to plan the games and secondly, because they had actually enjoyed it!

God has been showing us principles that the modern world has abandoned. He has told us about honesty at work; integrity in our employment; a proper work ethic with workmen doing a good day's work and honouring their bosses; bosses being honest instead of manipulating the labour in order to get the best out of them and destroying them in the process. The Bible teaches responsibility on every side. These are the wonderful laws of the kingdom – the wisdom of God for how to live on His planet.

We have also been learning how to be a covenant-keeping community in an age where covenant is easily cast aside. We are finding joy through living righteously in a world that is as miserable as sin – we ought to use this phrase frequently! Let's talk about being "as miserable as sin" so that people will hear and understand that *sin is essentially miserable* and that God has caused us to find joy through righteousness! Tragically, unbelievers have often regarded Christians as killjoys. It is time that they discovered that we are "have-joys"!

When Joseph was confronted by the prospect of famine he stored up everything the people would need to see them through the national emergency. Similarly, God is storing up all the necessary resources in His Church. He has given us kingdom principles and He has shared His own wisdom with us.

Open the storehouses

Joseph fulfilled his calling by opening up his storehouses to minister to the nation's needs. As the famine spread over all the face of the earth, Joseph threw open Egypt's vast resources (see Genesis 41:56). The nation was in dire need and Joseph had all the answers so the people poured in to buy grain from him.

Joseph was truly a prophetic figure. We started our story by noting that in the last days, *"Your old men will dream dreams, your young men will see visions"* (Joel 2:28 NIV). But we should also notice that:

> *"Now it will come about that*
> *In the last days*
> *The mountain of the house of the LORD*
> *Will be established as the chief of the mountains,*
> *And will be raised above the hills;*
> *And all the nations will stream to it.*
> *And many peoples will come and say,*
> *'Come, let us go up to the mountain of the LORD,*
> *To the house of the God of Jacob;*
> *That He may teach us concerning His ways*

And that we may walk in His paths.'
For the law will go forth from Zion
And the word of the LORD from Jerusalem.
And He will judge between the nations,
And will render decisions for many peoples."

                                        (Isaiah 2:2–4)

There it is! In the last days God will cause the mountain of
the house of the Lord, that great Zion about which we so often
sing, to be raised above the other mountains. The "other"
mountains will not be able to come up with the answers –
political, economic or social. Whatever their philosophies,
they will not be able to provide answers. But the mountain
of the Lord will appear above the other mountains and the
nations will say, "There is grain there. Those Christians
have found how to live. Let us go!" God has promised that
this will happen. The unsaved will say, *"Let us go up to the*
mountain of the LORD . . . that He may teach us about His ways"
(Micah 4:2).

It will be those whose marriages are in desperate straits, who
don't know how to look after their children, who are in
financial trouble and who are confronted by so many different
problems – they'll seek us out. Ordinary people like you and
me, who have been through the furnace, through the testing,
will be seen as corporate testimony in our towns. And
people will come and ask us how we are happy and fulfilled,
and how it is that our families are so secure.

Isaiah 60:1–5 underlines the same amazing promise:

"Arise, shine, for your light has come,
And the glory of the LORD has risen upon you.
For behold, darkness will cover the earth
And deep darkness the peoples . . . "

(This is another way of saying that there is going to be a vast moral famine.)

> *"But the* LORD *will rise upon you*
> *And His glory will appear upon you.*
> *Nations will come to your light,*
> *And kings to the brightness of your rising.*
>
> *Lift up your eyes round about and see;*
> *They all gather together, they come to you.*
> *Your sons will come from afar,*
> *And your daughters will be carried in the arms.*
> *Then you will see and be radiant,*
> *And your heart will thrill and rejoice . . . "*

In the last days God will bring forth a marvellous, mature, "Joseph company" with answers for the famine. People will stream in.

Even Joseph's own brothers began to hear. He was no longer perceived to be arrogant, an over-confident teenager flaunting his spiritual visions. He now appeared with maturity and wisdom, having grain in the midst of famine.

Brotherly love triumphs!

How did Joseph fulfil his calling? He graciously received his brothers. Indeed, the way in which he received them is one of the most beautiful parts of the whole story. He did not turn on them, nor did he say, "You threw me out and now I have the upper hand!" No, Joseph was genuinely thrilled that his brothers wanted to come. There was no resentment, no bitterness, no keeping them at arm's length. He loved them.

At first he did not reveal his identity, but when he saw them his heart went out to them and he was so moved that he quickly left the room to weep in private. Eventually the moment came for disclosure: "I am Joseph, your brother." Amazed and fearful they backed away, fearing his revenge, but he called them to come closer and reassured them: *"As for you, you meant evil against me, but God meant it for good in order to bring about this present result, to preserve many people alive"* (Genesis 50:20). Then Joseph threw his arms around them and kissed them, and they wept and talked together.

Some of you may have been asked to leave churches because you have seen visions, prophesied or spoken with tongues. Will you be as open as Joseph? God's purpose was for all his sons; His plans were for the whole nation of Israel. It was, in fact, from *Judah*, rather than Joseph, that God's ultimate purpose would emerge.

Do not think that because you have had a vision you are special. No! God sent a man ahead that He might save them all. His heart was for all His beloved children whether they receive your visions and dreams or not and whether they accept your testimony or not. God's heart is for everyone whom He has purchased with the blood of His Son, for He loves every one and sees all partaking in His glorious purpose.

In recent years a growing number have stepped out of the clutter of irrelevant tradition and, unrestricted by lifeless formality, they have been freed to rediscover some of the basic essentials required for building a church that will reach a generation. The world is already beginning to say, "These churches really speak my language; they are not pushing religion at me – they have something I want. They seem to love each other; they are a community, sharing their posses- sions and giving to one another; their faith does not seem to be confined to special buildings on special days." Growing numbers are beginning to be saved and are sharing this kind of a testimony.

Joseph was able to feed the people in a time of famine, but this was not all: Psalm 105:21 says quite plainly that Pharaoh made him lord of his house and ruler over all his possessions, with authority to imprison Pharaoh's princes at will. Joseph exercised real authority in Pharaoh's world.

God is not simply raising up His Church to feed the nations; He is bringing in a kingdom where Jesus is Lord. The people of God are to be formed into an army that wages spiritual warfare and learns to *"bind their kings with chains and their nobles with fetters of iron, to execute on them the judgment written; this is an honour for all His godly ones"* (Psalm 149:8–9). The Church must demonstrate the rule and government of Christ.

Even now we are seated with Christ in heavenly places on His throne, sharing His authority. God told His Son long ago, *"Sit at My right hand until I make Your enemies a footstool for Your feet"* (Psalm 110:1). (The Old Testament verse that is most quoted in the New Testament.)

Jesus will be seen as a mighty King in and through His people, with Him as our head in heaven and with His people on earth. People will come from every nation to hear the ways of God. Jesus is the Saviour of *all* men, especially those who believe (see 1 Timothy 4:10). All men, not just believers, will benefit from the vast reservoirs of God's grace just as Egypt benefited from Joseph's lifesaving work.

We are reminded in 1 Corinthians 15:24–25 that one day Jesus will return:

> *"Then comes the end, when He hands over the kingdom to the God and Father, when He has abolished all rule and all authority and power. For He must reign until He has put all His enemies under His feet."*

What a glorious consummation of the ages when there is a worldwide expression of the government of Jesus and then He hands over the rule to His Father, having subjected all authority to Himself. By God's grace let us be partners with Him in His great plan of redemption and bring everlasting glory to the Lamb!

PART 2

Gideon

"... *whose weakness was turned to strength;*
and who became powerful in battle
and routed foreign armies."
(Hebrews 11:34 NIV)

Sitting in Darkness

The sky was black. The passengers dozed uncomfortably as the plane flew on through the night. I lifted the blind and stared out at the dense darkness. Gradually, I became aware that a change was taking place. It was as if someone had taken a razor blade and made a gigantic cut on the eastern horizon. An orange line appeared and as the perfectly straight line widened, light poured through in an increasing intensity of golden brilliance. Dawn was breaking across the sky, overcoming the night.

"The people who walk in darkness will see a great light." So begins one of the best-known prophecies in Isaiah. As it continues a picture unfolds of a time when God's nation shall be multiplied, the yoke of slavery broken, and a new government will emerge.

It will be an ever-increasing government, resting comfortably on the shoulders of a child born to us whose name will be called Wonderful Counsellor, Mighty God, Everlasting Father, Prince of Peace, and there will be no end to the increase of His government (see Isaiah 9:2–7). Wonderful promises herald the coming of the King and His kingdom.

We live in days of the kingdom's advance. Jesus said that this gospel of the kingdom must be preached to all nations before the end comes. Through the ages men and women have carried the baton in their generation. Now our time has come. Ultimately the light of the kingdom will be seen by all the nations who sit in darkness. A time of significant breakthrough must come!

But how will it come? What can we expect? Isaiah 9:4 gives us an unexpected clue when it tells us it will be *"as at the battle of Midian."* So, if we want to find out how light overcomes darkness, and what happens when the light of God explodes into a world that has grown accustomed to shadows, confusion and blindness, we need to look at this battle of Midian. Here we shall discover important lessons that are particularly relevant today as we look for God's power to break out through the spiritual darkness of our own generation.

At that time the Israelites were also "living in darkness" (see Judges 6). They were in hiding, overwhelmed by their enemies and lacking any sense of the blessing of God resting upon them. However, by the end of chapter 7 the defeated nation has been transformed into a victorious people. Clearly, these chapters contain crucially important principles which we cannot afford to overlook.

The story begins with a description of one of the most devastating scenes of Israel in the Old Testament. They lived in constant fear of the raiding Midianite armies: repeated savage attacks had eventually forced them into hiding and they began living in mountain caves. Every time they planted seeds in the valley their enemies would invade and destroy the entire crop. The once conquering nation of Israel had therefore gradually fallen into a period of terrible decline and it seemed as though the enemies of Israel were invincible; nothing could be done about them. Before long the Israelites had to adapt to just simply existing under great pressure and eventually they resorted to hiding.

Now, the tragedy in Gideon's day was that this people, these sons of Israel, were God's people. They were a people of great destiny and of a magnificent past. The previous generations under Moses and Joshua had known outstanding victories and triumphs, and they had experienced many outbreaks of the supernatural power of God: they had seen the Red Sea separate and they had seen the walls of Jericho crumble. This was their immediate history. They also had a glorious future. The next generation would see the anointing of Samuel, leading to the mighty kingdoms of David and Solomon.

However, during the period spanned by the book of Judges there was a desperate spiritual drought – a tragic time between a miraculous past and a brilliant future. It was tragic because it was also a charismatic era when God showed Himself willing to pour out His Spirit on individuals. What a tragedy to live in such a time, amongst a people of such calling, who were without purpose or hope. God's power was available to them and yet they lived without any obvious sense of His blessing.

How relevant this story is to the Church in our nation today. We are seen as an irrelevant body, lacking both strength and purpose; a tiny percentage of the population; a remnant from a previous age. A national newspaper recorded its appraisal of the modern minister as this: "He is a general dogsbody looking after a group of well-meaning but generally harmless people."

This is hardly how the New Testament describes the Church but, nonetheless, most people will settle for this in describing today's Church.

In today's Church people are looking at the serious needs of our land but arriving at so many different solutions. As in Gideon's day, the truth that was formerly believed and obeyed has been abandoned and men are doing what they see as right in their own eyes. A minister recently told me that he attended a local conference for his particular denomination where it was suggested that the reason people do not attend churches any more is because we are so full of ourselves; that we arrogantly invite people to come and hear us and that surely we could change and say that all men are seeking God. It was said that we should invite non-Christians to discussions instead of services and share ideas in our common search for God. To my friend's horror the suggestion was received with much enthusiasm! They thought that this was a great idea!

Most people regard today's Church as hopelessly outdated, offering no relevant answers. Meanwhile, our enemies are gaining ground – at least it would appear so. In my hometown of Brighton there have been major spiritualist conferences and conventions for all manner of groups involved in the occult. We see our enemies gaining ground while the Church remains insignificant, apparently with no answers and with no word for the situation, just hiding in caves.

However, in this nation we can also look back to times when God has moved powerfully. Many Christians also believe that He will do so again, for we are convinced that it is God's purpose to bring His Church to the fullness of the stature of Christ. We are confident that God is going to prepare His Bride until she is without spot or wrinkle, ready for Jesus. We have been privileged with a wonderful history and a glorious future awaits us. Are we content to just live in a spiritual trough and fail to believe for a move God in our generation?

This is the setting for the story of Gideon and God has made special mention of it in Isaiah 9. The marvellous increase of government shall be *"as the battle of Midian"*.

How it all began

It all started during a time of spiritual decline, but first we must see just how and why the nation arrived at such a low point. A simple explanation could be that the Midianites were too strong an enemy and, overwhelmed, the Israelites retreated to the caves. This is the *simple* answer.

A more sophisticated interpretation that has been put forward in some commentaries is that they had been defeated by a secret new weapon which they had never encountered before – a new problem that they had never faced! This secret weapon had great speed and the ability to strike at great speed. It was the camel! The Midianite army, with the aid of camels, presented problems that Israel had never before encountered in warfare. It was because of the camel, some would have us believe, that Israel fell into decline.

Actually, if we look closely we find that neither the Midianite nation nor their "secret weapon" provide us with the real answer. It would be lunacy to assume that the God who dealt with the Red Sea and mighty Jericho had found His match in a camel! No. The fact that Israel was overrun was a demonstration that their problem was not with the Midianites at all, but with God Himself.

The real problem

Judges 6 begins:

> *"Then the sons of Israel did what was evil in the sight of the* Lord; *and the* Lord *gave them into the hands of Midian seven years."*

It was not that their enemies were too great, but rather that God was not with them. More than this it says in Judges 2:15, *"Wherever they went, the hand of the* Lord *was against them for evil..."* Therefore God was actively against His own people. It further says, *"the* Lord *strengthened Eglon king of Moab against*

Israel" (Judges 3:12). In reading the Old Testament we find that
God often strengthened Israel's pagan enemies when Israel
turned away from Him – a fact that bewildered Habbakuk and
a truth that Jeremiah had to live with throughout his entire
ministry.

The Israelites were therefore defeated and living in caves –
not because God's strength was insufficient to help them – but
because God was so mighty! Ruling in heaven and on earth, He
was strengthening their enemies!

What about today?

How do these circumstances speak to our situation today? Some
would argue that the Church is not prospering today because of
new problems that we have never had to face before. We have to
contend with the vast pressure of a secular society, humanist
teaching in schools and continual brainwashing by the media.
Some would list other modern-day "camels" that prevent the
Church from prospering such as secularism, pluralism and
rampant atheism. Some feel that the Church simply cannot cope
with the problems of the twenty-first century. The implication is
that somehow God cannot keep up with modern trends!

Scripture, however, teaches us something very different,
namely that God will even strengthen enemies against His
people when they are not honouring Him. We must not be
tempted to think that this is a situation confined to the Old
Testament. God has never said that He will be with His people
in any circumstance and at all costs.

Our God is a holy God. He gives His Holy Spirit to *those who
obey Him*. He answers the prayers of the righteous and He will
cause the devil to flee if we humble ourselves before Him. We
know that God gives grace to the humble and that He opposes
the proud! This truth is written in a letter to His own people.

God will oppose the proud. He will also oppose lying and cheating – even in His New Testament Church. He removed Ananias and Sapphira for this very reason. Paul wrote to the church at Corinth, *"Some of you are sick and some have even died"* when they abused the Lord's Supper. God judged them. The Church in sin does not merely miss out on blessing but actually experiences the opposition of Almighty God.

So often we assume that it is the devil who closes down churches. When we hear of church buildings being converted into warehouses or bought by other religions we regard it as the devil's work. But the New Testament says that Jesus stands in the middle of the candlesticks and says, "I will remove this one and close that one." God has never left His throne! He is to be feared. He will have His people as they are meant to be, otherwise He will oppose them, and He does not just dole out blessings without a care!

As the government of Jesus increases God will have deep dealings with His people. Jesus is not just gentle and mild – He is also the God of wrath and judgement. For example, look at the early chapters of the book of Revelation. Old Testament or New, He remains the same true God.

If you read through the second chapter of Revelation, in which Jesus is speaking to His churches, you see such words of judgement as:

> *"But I have this against you, that you have left your first love. Therefore remember from where you have fallen, and repent and do the deeds you did at first; or else I am coming to you and will remove your lampstand out of its place."*
>
> (Revelation 2:4–5)

Jesus goes on to threaten war, sickness and tribulation against the various churches if they refuse to repent.

This is our mighty God. We cannot just carry on as we want and hope that God will bless us. Neither can we plead special excuses for the difficult days in which we live. How many people have you met who say, "Of course our town is a very difficult one – a real centre for witchcraft"? No town is too difficult for God. He stands above it all. The Lord Jesus said, *"All authority has been given to Me in heaven and on earth"* (Matthew 28:18). But He also said, *"I have this against you . . ."*

This was the situation in Gideon's day. Their defeat was not due to the power of the enemy at all! God had some things against them.

God also has some things against today's Church which He is putting right. We need to know what they are and respond diligently. There are two possibilities open to us when God isn't blessing us: we can either settle for the status quo, or we can cry out to God.

Another generation

In Gideon's day there were those who chose to just get used to the situation. They really had not known, firsthand at least, that it could be any different. A tragic phrase in Judges 2 shows us that those of the great generation who had seen Jericho fall were all dead:

> *"All that generation also were gathered to their fathers; and there arose another generation after them who did not know the* LORD, *nor yet the work which He had done for Israel."*
>
> (Judges 2:10)

They themselves had never seen His power manifest.

On the whole we too have grown up in a generation that has not seen the mighty acts of God as our forefathers did. We have not seen revivals during which thousands flock into the churches to get right with God. Unlike our fathers we have not known whole towns change, with demonstrations of power and incredible manifestations of the glory of God. The majority of our generation knows nothing of these things so we may closely identify with the Israel of Gideon's day.

Finding that God was not with them, many of His people simply dug in, living in holes on the mountains. It was even more pitiful than this because mountains are supposed to typify significant places for strategic possession. When they had begun to move into the Promised Land under Joshua the mountains represented the heights of authority and power.

Caleb, for his reward, sought a mountain. To be on top of a mountain in warfare was to be in the place of great authority. The mountains also feature in psalms of praise: get up into a high mountain and say, "Behold your God." The mountains were to be possessed, but instead this generation of Israel dug in and *"prepared shelters for themselves in mountain clefts, caves and strongholds"* (Judges 6:2 NIV).

In a similar way you can either possess a great truth of God or you can dig in and hide behind it. There were people who did this in Jesus' day. They said, "We are children of Abraham." To them Abraham was a mountain figure of faith, but unlike Abraham, they never knew the faith that he'd had. When Jesus came to them He ushered in a new day of the Spirit, a new demonstration of the power of God. Yet they said, "No, we are sons of Abraham, we received the law from Moses." They might have said, "No, our doctrine is sound."

Likewise, we often take great truths from the Bible and instead of living in the good of them we dig in defensively and hide behind them. The result is that instead of saying, "God is faithful; let us therefore bring the kingdom," we say, "God is faithful; I will defend that truth to the end."

When I was at Bible college we were taught that the main objective was to be "sound". We were sound and we were going to show the modern liberal theologians where they were not sound! We were also taught to beware of any undue emphasis of doctrine. We were safe and careful and the key word was "balance". If anybody got too excited they were moving into emotionalism. As a friend of mine wrote mockingly in a college magazine, "As we worship this great God of soundness and balance, with both feet firmly on the ground, let us go forward."

We find that the "sound" men of Jesus' day were always on the defensive. They took offence at the disciples' neglect of ceremonial washings. Time after time they spoke out against Jesus as they sought to protect the truth as they understood it, the rules behind which they hid.

By contrast, in Caleb's day, they laid hold of the truth. They argued, "If God is faithful, as the Word says, let us go and take the land." Their doctrine was a source of confidence – more a springboard than a dugout! However, Gideon's generation, not having seen God's power themselves, fell into the temptation to hide in the mountain caves. There is no time for "digging in" defensively. It's time to get onto the offensive and take God at His word.

However, we must firstly put our own house in order. Our individual lives must come under scrutiny and so must the way in which we run the Church of the Living God. I believe that God wants His Church back! He wants it to be run in His own way.

May God deliver us from defending cold orthodoxy. Instead, let us *be* orthodox like Caleb, by obeying God and proving Him as we believe His infallible Word and put it into action.

CHAPTER 10

The Prophet Explains

If to "dig in" is one option when God is not blessing the Church, the other option is to simply cry out to God. But what should we cry? Today there are many who are beginning to cry to the Lord – a great body of prayer warriors is beginning to stir up across the nation – but what should we pray?

Should we pray, "God smash the Midianites"? Jesus' contemporaries wanted to pray, "O God, break the Roman yoke." Like this we might be tempted to pray, "O Lord, break through against the atheists, the pluralists" or whatever. But this is not the prayer that God is waiting to hear, for it is not where the problem lies. What they ought to have prayed for, and what we must seek God for, is revealed in the answer that He gave. When they began to cry out to God He supplied three answers: a prophetic explanation, an anointed leadership and a committed army. This was God's response then and this is also what He wants to do now.

Praying against spiritualists or occult conferences can be seen as only attacking pimples on the surface. Our problem is not simply with the enemy; our problem is with God, who wants to speak to us through a prophetic voice. This is what He did in David's day. He sent the prophet Samuel, who in turn anointed fresh leadership before a committed army who were gathered under David. The formula was repeated in Jesus' day: first came John the Baptist, then our anointed Saviour and ultimately, the committed army.

The prophetic message brought to Gideon's generation reminded them that firstly they were a covenant people. He said, "I brought you out of Egypt. I delivered you against powerful forces. The Egyptians were far too powerful for you, so I delivered you and brought you into the land – but you have not obeyed Me. You did not drive out your enemies."

Throughout the book of Judges God repeatedly challenged them. Although God had performed such wonders for His people, they had not obeyed Him. They were supposed to drive out the enemy forces with all their evil practices, but Israel instead learned to live with them. After a while, we find that they were not only coexisting with the Canaanites, but also worshipping their gods. Spiritual adultery! They were meant to come into the land, purge the land of evil and establish the kingdom of God. Instead they settled, got used to the evil going on around them and eventually accepted these standards. Worst of all, they grieved the Lord by bowing down to Amorite idols (see Judges 6:10), the false gods of that age.

God would raise the same issues with His Church today. Our present weakness and lack of power is not so much to do with the strength of our enemies; it is to do with our spiritual adultery. Our God remains the same holy God and He would say, "Deliver yourselves from the gods all around you. Step right out and be a people for Me and you will see My power and glory in your own day."

Modern idols

What are the false gods that we worship today? There are many but I would like to mention just two or three specifically.

Money dominates today's society. So many people spend their lives and energies striving for more and more. During the Sermon on the Mount Jesus said quite simply that you cannot serve God and money. If you serve money you will eventually be trapped in the cares of this world and they will preoccupy you, bringing you into bondage.

Jesus said, *"For where your treasure is, there your heart will be also"* (Matthew 6:21). How many of us who say, "Money has no power over me" would give up the offer of promotion and prospects in another region in order to remain where God is using us? If the offered job is in a town where there is no dynamic, living, Spirit-filled fellowship, will you go? It is easy to say, "There's bound to be a church there," but we all know that in these days that there are lots of churches. It is easy to say, "We'll see what we can find when we get there," but this is actually putting the kingdom of God second. Jesus told us to seek first the kingdom of God and His righteousness (see Matthew 6:33). Do we make our decisions according to His standards or according to the standards all around us?

We have seen those who have put their careers first and as a result have lost their way. Their spiritual lives have declined and their children have grown up robbed of a living church.

Our heart attitude regarding money is also tested by our reaction to giving. Many say, "What with inflation and my mortgage, and other financial commitments, I can't really afford to give. I give what I can, but tithing is ridiculous." But Jesus said, *"Give, and it will be given to you ... a good measure – pressed down, shaken together, and running over"* (Luke 6:38).

Jesus said, "Do not fear – give!" It's a different way of life. It defies the gods of this world. The gods of this world warn you to hold on or you will be in a terrible state when you get to the end of the month. Jesus, however, is a different kind of king. He says, "Give and it will be given to you." He says that those who obey these words will have solid rock foundations to their lives and not treacherous sands. God has written principles that defy the world. Proverbs 11:24 says,

> *"There is one who scatters, and yet increases all the more,*
> *And there is one who withholds what is justly due,*
> *and yet it results only in want."*

Those who say, "I can't give at the moment, I can't afford it" are not responding to the voice of God, but are responding to the gods of this world.

Kingdom treasure

The kingdom of God is like a man who found treasure in a field and said, "I'll sell everything else I have in order to possess that field. Everything else must go. I must have the treasure. I must have the kingdom of God. I want to be in the kingdom where God moves with power. I want to see the demonstration of the glory of Jesus. I want my dear Saviour who bled and died and was exalted and glorified. I want to be in His kingdom. I am not going to throw it away by making secular considerations. I have found something that is worth everything, that's the pearl of great price, and I will let everything go to obtain it; everything in order to be in the centre of His will."

How is it with you? That's the standard that Jesus talked about. He said that this is how it is when people follow Him. He gave everything to possess us and He wants us to show the same response. He wants a Bride caught up in the magnitude of His love, not a people ensnared in the cares of this world.

One of the things that God used to provoke me into full-time ministry was a meeting with a young Jehovah's Witness. He was financing himself by window cleaning each morning so that he could go out knocking on doors with his message in the afternoons. I thought, "Here am I, giving all my time to work and travelling to work, but this fellow has given everything to serve in a miserable cult."

God is looking for a whole army that will arise with this clear priority: the pearl that is above price. Our goal is not how much we can get away with, or how much we can hold on to. It's not, "Shall I tithe before or after tax?" nor is it seeking your career, your home or your prospects first. It is a totally different attitude. Jesus said that if we cannot be clear about this we will never make progress with Him, for we cannot serve both God and money.

Preoccupation with sex

The second powerful god around us today was also worshipped in Gideon's generation. The goddess Ashtoreth, among other evil practices, was a goddess of sexual perversion. Our generation is also obsessed by sex and numberless lives are held in its grip.

I have heard some younger people say, "But it's so hard today. Everyone talks about it at school. I get laughed at. Only two or three of us in my class are still virgins. I do mean to marry my boyfriend one day and I'm sure that God understands. I suppose we have let the standards drop a bit."

God's standards have never changed and yet so many in His Church have given in to the pressure to follow the world. So many have let their purity go because of an ugly, ensnaring god that prevails in our land today. But God has given us everything we need for life and godliness (see 2 Peter 1:3). We must not, and need not, serve other gods. God wants us to be free. He wants us to be holy. He wants our standards to be bright and clear.

Of course, it's not only the young who are pressured by this god. People in their middle years will often have to face new areas of temptation and pressure. People with unconverted husbands or wives find warmth of friendship with other Christians in the Church. Suddenly and unexpectedly they can find themselves lured and under pressure. But God will not own a people who bow down to this god.

In the book of Revelation Jesus spoke against a church that tolerated adultery. His burning gaze penetrated the situation. With a sword proceeding from His mouth He will deal with His Church regarding the worship of other gods. He sees it as spiritual adultery. It is obeying the power of the world, following its gods, giving in to its ways.

Jesus is seeking faithfulness among His people, His Bride. We must live in purity before Him. God wants us to be free from this ugly god of sexual sin that stalks our land. He wants His people to be holy and free. It is not enough for us to say, "Everyone else is doing it." We have got to be free. Young people especially, you must stand up in these days and be free from these pressures through God's power.

Foolish wisdom

The third god that confronts us is "worldly wisdom", a god that has always attempted to creep into the Church. Paul spelled out the enmity between the gospel and worldly wisdom, teaching that the gospel of the cross is folly to the world – it is foolishness! The worldly wise man of today thinks he has outgrown a gospel of a cross and shed blood. He would much rather speak philosophically; he is too sophisticated for such primitive nonsense!

A god of worldly wisdom is in some ways a subtle one and yet how willingly many Christians yield to its pressure. Because some of the things God speaks of in His Word are not easily understood, we begin to cut our cloth. Rather than be out-spoken with the foolishness of our message we make things acceptable for the modern man.

Many are doing this today, even with the current outpouring of the Holy Spirit. They speak in tongues and rejoice in new experiences, but they restrict them to discreet midweek meetings. Meanwhile, Sunday services are unchanged; a nice, ordered service that's calculated to offend no one. That is where worldly wisdom comes in – don't offend, let's be quiet; let's keep it played down!

The Bible contains so much that is offensive to the intellect, yet God has called us to wholehearted commitment to His truth, to the cross, to the outpouring of the Spirit and to the Church coming to fullness of stature.

In Gideon's day, when they gave themselves to the worship of other gods, God's prophetic word to them was, "I will not own you until you put these things right." It is also His word to us today. God will never say, "If they can't do what I require I will drop the standards and bless them." He will simply wait for another generation. This does not prove that God is weak. He is not thrown if someone scrawls on the wall, "God is dead", because he sits as King forever! We can get anxious about it, but Jesus is King and, if necessary, He will wait for another generation. God will have a people who live according to His standard that He might display them for His glory and honour.

Embrace the cross

God wants us to be free from this world. How do we get free? There is only one way and this is through the cross of our Lord Jesus Christ. The apostle Paul said, *"May it never be that I should boast, except in the cross of our Lord Jesus Christ"* (Galatians 6:14). He did not say, "I boast in the memory of it." He did not even

say, "I boast in the cross as I consider what Jesus did for me."
He said, *"May it never be that I should boast, except in the cross of
our Lord Jesus Christ, through which the world has been crucified to
me, and I to the world."* He glorified in it experientially. He said,
in effect, "This cross has released me from the world. It has
delivered me from the gods all around me. I now live to God as
one alive from the dead."

The cross is not something to glory in as a memory. It is a
mighty, powerful instrument on our lives that sets us free.
Through it we died to these gods in order that we might rise up
holy, free and pure.

Is this the way that you are living?

God's prophetic word to us toady is exactly the same as it was
in the days of the Judges. He is saying, "I am your covenant
God. I brought you out of Egypt, but you are worshipping other
gods. You make your decisions before them and not before Me."
As in the book of Revelation, Jesus says to us, "I have this against
you." Prophet after prophet in the Old Testament thundered
out this word. They spoke continually against compromise.
Elijah said, *"How long will you waver between two opinions? If the
LORD is God, follow him"* (1 Kings 18:21 NIV).

If we will hear this word now and respond as Gideon did,
then God will move once more. It only needs a small company
to obey at first. God said in Isaiah that the increase of His
government will be, *"as at the battle of Midian"* (Isaiah 9:4). This
was a time when a small company of people heard the prophet,
followed anointed leadership and committed themselves to the
army. This is all that God needs. This is all that He is waiting
for; then He can turn the land upside down.

We don't need to pray about the Midianites and their camels,
or whatever the modern equivalents might be. We need to
respond to the prophetic word.

Finding the Right Man

Following the prophet's word, God, in His great mercy, began to provide His answer. Firstly, He sent an angel. It is particularly interesting to note that God did not send His angels to defeat the Midianites, but to speak to a man.

An angel may be empowered to do great and mighty things, but God has committed His purpose to men and women and does not ultimately bypass them. However black the situation is God does not say, "I will have to work by My angel power this time." In these days of spiritual darkness God is still looking for men and women that He can work through.

We read that the angel who was sent to Gideon was actually "the angel of the Lord" – this same angel of the Lord who appeared to Joshua and Abraham – the pre-incarnate Lord Jesus found Gideon. The angel of the Lord, whose mere breath could have destroyed Midian unaided, was selecting his chosen instrument.

In John 15:5 Jesus says, *"I am the vine; you are the branches . . . apart from me you can do nothing"* (NIV). The amazing implication of this is that He is also saying that since we are His branches He does nothing without us; not because He lacks sovereign power, but because He has chosen to accomplish His purposes on earth through the people He loves.

What kind of man?

One might imagine that God would seek out a powerful, dynamic leader from among His people. It was, after all, a fairly hopeless situation. The Israelites were living a beggarly existence, hiding in caves and constantly threatened by savage Midianite raids. One might expect that God would be looking for an identifiable national hero, a focus for His people's aspirations; ideally someone strong, courageous, persuasive, influential, clear-sighted and determined.

But the angel of the Lord found Gideon. Was it a joke or had he made a mistake? Did he not know, Gideon wondered, that he had just approached the least significant member of the least significant family of the least significant tribe in all Israel? Gideon was a nobody, so why was he chosen?

We, however, should be less surprised at God's choice than Gideon was. Scripture teaches us that very often God calls the young, the unqualified and the inexperienced into His service.

When God sent Samuel to Jesse's household to anoint the future king, Samuel met many tall, good looking, accomplished young men but God kept saying "No" until the youngest appeared. This was the young boy David, who had been out in the field looking after a few sheep. Nobody had considered him, but he was God's choice – the youngest and the least.

Similarly, we read that Jeremiah considered himself too young. The apostle Paul had to encourage Timothy not to let men despise his youth and Joseph and David were both young men when God laid hold of their lives. So too was Samuel.

Gideon, however, was different from the other young men that God called. Whereas the others had much to commend them, Gideon did not. David may have been young and inexperienced, but he had killed a lion and fought a bear. He knew and loved God, and worshipped Him with his harp.

Although he was young he was full of zeal and faith, and was unafraid to face Goliath.

Daniel may also have been young, but he was a man of integrity and clarity; a man of determined purpose. They both had things to commend them, but Gideon seemed to have nothing to commend him at all. Not only was he insignificant, he was totally insecure.

The feeblest saint

Joseph, as a young man, saw visions. Gideon only saw problems! He was just a feeble, insecure man. Look at the way he responded to the call of God: He said, "If it is you speaking to me I'll just go and prepare something for you." So he prepared a meal and put it on the rock. The angel of the Lord then touched it with his rod and it vanished in smoke, where-upon the angel also disappeared. Any one of us would have thought, "That clinches it, it really is God!" But no, this was not enough for Gideon.

Later on, even after God had been speaking to him so clearly, we find the strange story of the fleece. He asked God to confirm His intentions once more by a miraculous sign: If the fleece he left overnight was wet with dew and the ground was bone dry, then he would know for sure. When he awoke the next morning and God had answered his prayer, even this was not enough. Still insecure, still uncertain, he reversed the sequence – "Let the rain be here and let it be dry there" – never satisfied!

Finally, just before the battle God said to Gideon, "You are still frightened so go down and listen to the enemy." With every sign from God rejected, Gideon then had to hear the truth from the lips of the enemies. He overheard his victory foretold in a dream and at last Gideon believed. This is the man

God chose! God's man of faith and power? You may have expected God to have found somebody quite different, but He actually used the weakest and the most insignificant man.

How often we say, "If only God would convert somebody in a position of political power. If only that TV personality, pop singer or footballer could come forward, then we could hear his testimony and hundreds of teenagers would be saved." But Scripture says again and again that God chooses whom He will!

Have a look in 1 Corinthians 1:26–29,

> "For consider your calling, brethren, that there were not many wise according to the flesh, not many mighty, not many noble; but God has chosen the foolish things of the world to shame the wise, and God has chosen the weak things of the world to shame the things which are strong, and the base things of the world and the despised God has chosen, the things that are not, so that He may nullify the things that are, so that no man may boast before God."

So often we point to factors that we think disqualify us when they are the very things that God is looking for! God sees us feeling so weak, but He has chosen the weak. We say, "I am hopeless, I am despised." God says, "That's exactly what I want. In this time of spiritual bleakness I want to do a very great thing and I must find weak people." Often the problem that God has with us is that we are too strong. We have too much to offer, while He is looking for vulnerable people. Blessed are the poor in spirit, for theirs is the kingdom of heaven.

Mighty man of valour

When God called Gideon a "mighty man of valour" it must have been one of the best jokes since Abram was renamed

Abraham. Abram had suffered the indignity of a totally inappropriate name, which means "exalted father"! He had struggled hard to live up to this name and God had to make it even worse! He renamed him Abraham, which means "father of a multitude". Abram was bad enough, but why Abraham?

We find that when God speaks, miracles are accomplished. Abraham eventually became what God had called him. When God speaks He calls things that are not as though they were. God created the heavens and the earth out of nothing, by the word of His power. He spoke and they sprang into being. And God would speak to us:

> *"Therefore, if anyone is in Christ, he is a new creature; the old things passed away, new things have come!"*
>
> (2 Corinthians 5:17)

He speaks and it is done. He said to Simon Peter, fully aware of all his weakness, "Simon, son of Jonah, you shall be Peter." Jesus spoke and this unstable man eventually became like a rock, living up to his name.

However, the man that God called "a mighty man of valour" was, at that point, still full of fear and insecurity. We may assume that he was also hurt because he said, "The Lord has abandoned us," which was not true. God will sometimes put us through very difficult times, allowing great pressures to come upon us to bring us into maturity, but He never, ever abandons us. And yet Gideon said, "The Lord has abandoned us." He was a wounded man as well as a weak man, and yet God still chose him.

God said, "There is one weak enough who won't be proud in my hands, one I can work through." No one is disqualified. God can pick up the frailest and use them.

Where are the miracles?

It would be wrong, however, to think that Gideon had nothing going for him. If he had no other strengths, he was a man thirsty for God. When the angel of the Lord addressed him he at least cared about the glory of God and the state of the nation. His response may have been weak, but at least it revealed how he felt about Israel's situation and how in his heart he longed for God to manifest His power. The angel's appearance provoked a torrent of questions: "Why has all this happened? Where are the wonders that our fathers spoke of when they told us that God rescued us from Egypt?" In all his weakness he was hungry for God.

How is it with you? Do you ask, "Lord, why is it like this – why is your Church so small? Where are all the miracles? Where is the great turning to you? Where is the demonstration that Jesus is alive?"

When Paul came to Athens and saw all the idolatry, his spirit was provoked within him. Are our spirits provoked within us, or have we come to settle? There must have been dispensationalists in Gideon's day. They probably said that it was in the "Joshua dispensation" that rivers opened up and walls fell down!

"Now, you have to understand that this was all in the past; this was just to get us into the land, just to get things going. Now we don't need miracles, now we are in the land – in hiding, yes, but we are in!"

Some of us have been raised up on such teaching. The power, the glory and the gifts of the Spirit were just to get the Church started. Now we have come to maturity, it is argued, we do not need these things. But Gideon rejected such ideas and longed for God's power to be seen. God looks for people like this, however weak they are. God does not despise your weaknesses, but He looks for soul thirst. He is not merely looking for those who know all the jargon, because commitment and obedience in themselves can be cold and routine. The people God delights in are those who cry out in their spirits, "I am hungry for God and I long to see Him!"

Moses said, *"If I have found favour in Your sight, let me know Your ways"* (Exodus 33:13). He was so hungry for God that even at the end of his life he said, "O God, You have only just begun to show me Your greatness." He had an appetite for God Himself. He did not just say, "Thank goodness I've found grace – let's sing some choruses about grace . . . " He saw that if he was in grace and that God was going to love him in spite of all his shortcomings, then perhaps God would reveal more of Himself. Although he had to carry the whole nation he still had time to get before God and say, "O God, show me Your glory." His desire was for God. His continual prayer was, "Let me see more of You. You are so wonderful. I am not content just leading Your flock through the wilderness to the Promised Land. I am not content merely to see Your great programme for them – I want to know You." God delights in people like this who are not just interested in what is happening to the Church at large, but are saying, "Oh God, I have a personal appetite for You."

Jacob, with all his weakness and faults also had an appetite for God. He was a crook, but he wanted God and God loved him and drew him on.

We are in great danger of superficiality, of routinely "doing the Lord's work" for no better reason than "there's work to be done". God desires a warmer relationship than that. Peter had many weaknesses, but at least he could say, "Lord, I have left everything to follow You." Can we say this?

We read of Nehemiah that when he heard about the situation in Jerusalem his heart was overwhelmed with grief.

Jerusalem's walls were in ruins and he wept and cried to God because he was zealous for Zion, zealous for the house of God.

God wants us to be such a people. Although we are weak and frail we are to be a people who are zealous for His house and who want to see the power of God manifest. This is the only qualification I can see in Gideon to start with – he had a hunger to see God at work.

Do you have a hunger to see God at work once more in power and glory? Or will you settle with the view that these are just quiet days for the Church – days to somehow muddle through, to survive, to hope for the best?

Sent by God

If weakness and spiritual hunger prepared Gideon for God's service, we must learn from this story that there was a third more important qualification. Gideon became a man *sent and commissioned by God*. He heard God say, "The Lord is with you. Go in this your strength and deliver Israel. Have not I sent you? Surely I will be with you."

A man who hears things like this from God has nothing to fear. A man who has heard this kind of promise has all heaven behind him. God's purpose must be established through such a person because his actions are not merely rooted in his own ideas. He is not simply responding to the need. He is not just saying, "I am not going to put up with this any more. I am going to go out after those Midianites," for he is not just a mere man moving on his own initiative. He has heard from God and God has laid hold of him. God will not necessarily own our activities, but if He has sent us we have His guarantee that He will own us as we do His bidding.

The need and the call

Some say, "The need constitutes the call. Because the mission field awaits we must go." But Jesus did not say, "Look, the harvest fields are white to harvest – *go*, therefore." He said, "The fields are white unto harvest. *Pray* therefore that the Lord of the harvest shall send forth His labourers – thrust them forth" (see Matthew 9:38 and John 4:35).

There is all the difference in the world between a man who sees the need and rushes into it wondering if God is with him and the man who, perhaps even reluctantly, has heard the call of God and goes knowing that God's hand is upon him.

Look at Moses! As a young and powerful prince in Egypt he saw a great need. His own people were oppressed and suffering in slavery and so he rushed in and killed an Egyptian. His best intentions went horribly wrong and he ended up having to flee. Why? Because *God did not send him.* Later on God said, "I have come down to deliver them and behold, I now send you." This was a different situation altogether. The same man was involved, but this time he was not rushing in to do what he could. God said, "I have seen the need and now I am sending you. I am the one who is doing the delivering."

This is how it had to be with Gideon. "I know your weakness," God said, "but I have sent you, therefore I am going to do it." It is never enough for us to say, "The need is there, we must rush to the need; we must answer the need" and hope that God agrees. We must hear what He says. The question arises, "Will they hear without a preacher?" and another question follows on its heels – "How will they go unless they are sent?"

When Paul's vision led him to Macedonia he ended up in prison. If he had not known in his heart that God had sent him the situation would have been devastating! As it was, he was full of praise and rejoicing because although his circumstances were dreadful, he knew he was right on course. Similarly, we sometimes find ourselves dogged by difficulties and pressures, but if we know we are where God has called us to be, then we can also rejoice. No matter how difficult our circumstances appear we can be at rest if we know that God has sent us.

I remember when I first heard a missionary appeal:

"Young men are needed on the mission field. Who will go?" The music played and all the women walked down the aisle! The preacher said, "Where are all the men who will go?"

I remember thinking, "Yes, of course, they need somebody like me; someone who will sort out a few things, get rid of some of the old fashioned ways, introduce some modern ideas. Here I am – just as I am – young, strong and free to be the best that I can!"

However, when the young Moses volunteered like this, God accepted him but then spent forty years preparing him in the wilderness!

Gideon did not even emerge as someone "young, strong and free"! Gideon came in all his weakness, but God apprehended him. He did not take it on himself to be able to do God's work simply because he was free and able. He went because God sent him.

It has been said that, "God has more problems with those who want to help Him than He has with backsliders!" We must wait for God to speak to us. The Israelites were under the Midianite yoke because of the very judgement of God. We must move in fear of God. If we blindly rush in, however good our intentions may be, the possibility always remains that we could actually be opposing the will of God. We must wait for Him to speak and then when He does, He will transform us into a people of faith.

By faith

It is to this aspect of faith that we must now turn our attention. Gideon was timid, fearful and weak, but through the call of God he was transformed into a man of real faith. It is scarcely believable, but Gideon appears in the Bible in Hebrews 11 – the great chapter of faith. One may be tempted to ask, "How on earth did he get there?" Gideon, of all people! Time did not permit the writer of Hebrews to go into detail about all those listed, but if we glance through verse 34 we read of one who, by faith, *"from weakness* [was] *made strong, became mighty in war, put foreign armies to flight."* Gideon, by faith, became strong out of weakness and qualified for Hebrews 11.

God sees you in your weakness and says, "O mighty man of valour, I'll get you into Hebrews 11! I'll get you into My book of heroes! I know what I can do with you in all of your frailty." Hallelujah! It thrills my heart. God can say this to any one of us in our weakness.

We must become men and women of faith. There is no other way, no bypass. It is nonsense to say, "I am too weak to become a man of faith." God doesn't despise your weakness, but He will not bless your unbelief. It is not enough to hear God's voice if we do not fully trust Him. Without faith it is impossible to please Him! We must not hide behind our weakness because when God says, "I have called you and now I send you" everything changes. You can become a person of real faith. However, if you do not respond to His word, if you continue to doubt and do not grow in faith, you will fail to do the work that God has called you to. The battle ahead for Gideon was going to be a battle of faith. The Israelites were not just outnumbered but faced ridiculous, impossible odds. The battle demanded faith and today's battles are no different. The whole Christian life is lived by faith.

If we do not respond in faith to God we will forever limit our activities to the things we can do in our natural strength. We argue, "This is something I *know* I can do" and as a result, fail to live by faith beyond our previous limitations. But God says that the just will live by faith and inevitably there will be times when He asks us to do things that are totally beyond our natural ability – things that we simply feel we cannot do! It might be leading in prayer, giving our testimony in public or door-to-door evangelism. The immediate response might well be like Gideon's: "You know me, I couldn't possibly do that!" But we will hold back God's work if we continue to only live within the restricted sphere of our own ability.

The rot sets in if we respond to God's promptings with self-doubt. Too often we evaluate fresh challenges by reference to our previous experience, our education, our personality, strength and ability. But God says, "By faith I want you to step right out of this. By faith come right out of your limitation." We will never turn the world upside down unless we begin living by faith.

God says, *"Do not fear, your worm Jacob ... I have made you a new threshing sledge with double edges; you will thresh the mountains ... "* (Isaiah 41:14–15). We do not have to stay as worms all the time. We must believe wholeheartedly and move beyond our previous limitations. Gideon became a man of faith and, even though it was with some trembling, he followed God. When God told him to destroy the altar of Baal, Gideon obeyed secretly and at night, supported by friends – but he did it! God prefers trembling obedience to bravado that has not even counted the cost.

We all respond with faith at the time of our conversion, but God wants us to live by faith all of the time.

Steps of faith

Years ago as a young Christian, when I was a commuter, I had a friend who went through every compartment on the Brighton to Victoria train giving out tracts. As you can imagine this is not a formula for popularity among sleeping or newspaper-reading commuters, but he did it. This brought me into complete condemnation because I knew it was something that I would never have the courage to do. However, some time later God said to me very clearly, "I want you to testify to the people in your compartment and give them tracts." I said, "Lord, I can't do that!" However, God had been showing me that I had to venture into situations beyond my own ability. He spoke to me from the story of Joshua where it says that when their feet actually touched the River Jordan it opened. When they actually stepped into it, God opened it.

In all probability I would have stood all day by the River Jordan. I may have even arranged nights of prayer and fasting as well, but as for putting my foot into the water before it opened, well, that would be scary! Many of us would have said, "O Lord, I'll pray all night!" but God said, "Put your foot in the water!" God says, "Move out of your areas of ability into My areas of ability. Let's see what I can do."

So, God said to me, "You give out tracts in your compartment." I said, "Lord, I can't do that, but what I can do is put the tracts in my pocket. That's as far as I can go." It was my way of putting my feet in the water, as it were. So I put the tracts in my pocket and I sat there on the train going from Brighton to London. When we got to Vauxhall Bridge (which is a far way on!) I finally *found myself* (I choose these words carefully) taking them out of my pocket. I found myself saying to the people in that compartment, "These are about Jesus. I would like you to read them as He has done so much for me." Afterwards, I sat there amazed. I suddenly found I could do the thing that I thought I could not do and for me it was a miracle!

Many of us limit what God is able to do simply by denying Him the opportunity to work. We flatly state, "I can't do that," effectively preventing Him from showing His power.

Gideon became strong by faith and if God can make a man like Gideon a man of faith, He can do it for anyone. He will not bless unbelief though. He loves even the faintest glimmer of genuine faith.

Trust and obey

The next thing we must learn about Gideon is that he was a man of obedience to God. In all his weakness he was obedient. God said, "Gideon, the first thing you have got to do is pull down that altar in your own home." He was first of all obedient to God at home.

One of the vital things that God is showing us today is that our obedience must first be demonstrated at this private level. Later on Gideon would stand up in battle and cry out, "Do as I do!" Leaders must also face the responsibility of saying, "Look at me and do likewise." So God warned Gideon, "Before I get you into such a place I have something to say to you about your home and the other god that is being worshipped there. Pull it down!" Any man or woman who is going to be used by God must get to grips with anything that is spoiling their life or home.

Maybe this will be costly. It was costly for Gideon – he risked the wrath of his father and of the city – but God said, "This is between you and Me, Gideon. Do it." Therefore, in all his weakness, together with a few friends around him, he obeyed God. He put himself in danger with those who were closest to him.

In Luke 12 Jesus said some words that He has never taken back from His commission to His Church:

"Do you suppose that I came to grant peace on earth? I tell you, no, but rather division; for from now on five members in one

> *household will be divided, three against two and two against*
> *three. They will be divided, father against son and son*
> *against father, mother against daughter and daughter against*
> *mother, mother-in-law against daughter-in-law and daughter-in-*
> *law against mother-in-law."*

(Luke 12:51–53)

If you are going to take this whole move of the Spirit seriously what will your family say? How will friends react? Will you press on after God? Is it in your heart to obey Him, however painful? God would say to us, "Will you go on with Me whatever the cost? No matter how weak, insecure and wounded you are, I can use you if you are obedient."

If you will obey God in your home and in your private world God will bless and own you, and develop His purpose in you. It could be that you will need help. You may need friends to stand with you just as Gideon did. But you must pull down all that offends God in your home life, whatever the cost. This cannot be bypassed no matter how tempting it is to try. The Lord will not own the man who says, "I'll be a leader but don't look too closely at my home." The altar to Baal must go first – and then see what God can do.

Peace with God

Gideon's quiet lifestyle was being revolutionised by this devastating encounter with God. Nevertheless, God loved him and had great plans for him, and so He spoke peace into his heart. He gave him a new revelation: Jehovah Shalom – God is peace.

We too must know this revelation. We need to know that God has taken away all our condemnation. God has dealt with the fear that comes upon us when we suddenly realise that we are dealing with God. When Gideon knew it was God he felt condemned. But God said, "Do not fear, you shall not die. I am the God who sends peace." When you are justified by faith you have peace with God and you cannot serve Him unless you have peace with Him. It is futile trying to serve God to prove yourself to Him, hoping that in some way you will perhaps improve in His estimation. He is Jehovah Shalom. He gives you peace on the grounds of His covenant relationship with you. He *gives* peace by His grace.

Gideon came to understand that God had accepted him and received him as he was. Gideon experienced this beautiful revelation – Jehovah Shalom – that the Lord gives peace. Do you know God's peace as you serve Him? It is so important to understand that we do not work for Him in the hope that He will eventually accept us. To believe this would be to live constantly in condemnation. Whether you succeed or fail the Lord gives peace. This peace is unconditionally yours on the grounds of His grace relationship with you!

Clothed with power

Finally, we read in Judges 6:34 that the Spirit of the Lord came upon Gideon, equipping him for the task. God's timing was perfect because Gideon came to faith and was filled with the Spirit at the very same time that the Midianites began to move in. It seems that they would raid whenever they felt that there was something worth destroying. As soon as the Israelites began to re-establish themselves, as soon as the fields began to produce again, the sons of the East would appear. The vast Midianite army would fill the horizon, sinking terror into the hearts of God's people. However, this time there was a man who had come to faith. Gideon, newly filled with the Spirit, came face to face with the real issue. This time the impossible was confronted by faith.

When the Virgin Mary was faced with the impossible as the angel told her what was to come she asked, "How can this be?" God's answer was, "The Spirit of the Lord shall come upon you." Similarly, when Gideon saw the huge armies assembling in the distance he might have asked, "How is this going to work?" God's solution has always been the same. The Spirit of the Lord "clothed" Gideon – or should we say "clothed himself with" Gideon. The result was a changed man – a man of power by the Spirit.

You will receive power when the Holy Spirit comes on you, as Scripture promises. This is God's answer in these dark days as He begins to stir us and kindle us. The wind is blowing on the dry bones. The Spirit of God is coming upon us in power and glory. The Holy Spirit is changing us, transforming us, giving us ability that we have never had before. It's releasing us from our fears, bringing us into freedom and power by His grace. Have you received the Holy Spirit since you believed? Have you been clothed with that power?

We are living in the age of the Spirit today. We are living in days when God says, "I will pour out My Spirit" – not on the occasional leader like Gideon; not on the occasional judge or king – "I will pour out My Spirit on all flesh. Your sons and daughters shall prophesy, your old men will dream dreams, your young men will see visions." God is pouring out His Spirit and every one of us can be filled by Him to move into battle.

The coming of the light of the kingdom will be like the battle of Midian. Be sure that you are prepared.

A Committed Army

As we have already seen in chapter 2, when God breaks powerfully into a situation it is often possible to observe a distinct pattern of events. First comes a prophetic explanation; secondly, God chooses and anoints leadership – in this case Gideon; thirdly, God calls together a committed army. We must turn to see what kind of army God uses because *we* are that army and Christ, not Gideon, is our captain. God is raising an army throughout the nations which is destined to be the most significant army the world has ever seen.

An army with faith

The first thing about Gideon's army was that it was an army that had faith. Not only was their leader a man of faith, each one had to have his own faith too. The first command was, "Let all who are fearful go home." This command was not just unique to this battle (see Deuteronomy 20:8), but it was doubly necessary on this occasion when they were so outnumbered.

If you can imagine this little company looking down the valley at the vast Midianite army and their camels, it is no wonder that Gideon needed a fearless army! Twenty-two thousand went home, so the steadfast that remained were not fearful, but men of faith.

Faith is the very opposite of fear. You cannot experience both at the same time. Jesus directed, "Fear not, only believe." God wants a people whose faith overcomes their fear. Often when preachers call us to greater commitment we find a question rising in our hearts: "But what if...?" Three small words born of fear. What will be the repercussions if I do this? How will I be thought of at home? What will they say? We persist in asking these questions while Scripture warns us that fear can steal so much of our inheritance.

When the Pharisees confronted Jesus regarding His authority He answered them with another question. He asked by what authority John baptized people. The Pharisees did not answer immediately, but began to weigh up the implications of their answers. If they had said, "By God's authority" Jesus could have asked, "Why then were you not baptized?" If they had said that John was not from God they knew they would incur the wrath of the people who commonly held John to be a prophet. So they said, "We do not know!" Rather than answer honestly they ducked a question that was too hot for them to handle!

In a similar way, some of us hear the word of God and weigh up the repercussions of what we are hearing. We say, "If I follow this, if I do that, such-and-such will happen..." We might agree with the preacher, but we are not ready for the implications. We weigh up the possible consequences of our alternative responses and end up being robbed by fear. The preaching moves us deeply time and time again, but we persist in saying, "I don't really know; I'm not sure."

Many went to hear John the Baptist preach – even the king went occasionally – just to witness the charisma of the mighty prophet. Similarly, Ezekiel spoke the word of God to vast crowds, but to them he was *"like a sensual song by one who has a beautiful voice and plays well on an instrument . . . "* (Ezekiel 33:32). But what does one who plays an instrument well accomplish? He thrills his audience with skilful playing and they praise the skill that's displayed, just as the singer of love songs moves hearts. But that is all. For a few moments people are moved, but not changed!

God wants us to be released from fear and to embrace His purposes. We must not think that Christianity is only for the naturally courageous any more than it is for the naturally brilliant. We know that God is for the smallest child so commitment is not only for the naturally tough guys! The naturally timid must not assume that they have no chance and might as well go home. If this were so, Gideon should have led the way home because he was the most fearful there.

Instead this story shows us that God can apprehend the naturally timid and transform them. The Church does not consist only of the courageous. It is for those who will respond to God and become strong, like Gideon, whether they are leaders or not. When God was looking for a young man to lead Israel through the River Jordan into the Promised Land He did not advertise in the *Wilderness Times*, "Wanted! Young man good at walking through rivers . . . " If He had He should have added, "No previous experience required"!

An army with courage

The Church must become bolder. Most of us have grown up in times where believers do not require much courage. But historically, whenever God has moved with power, there has always been a price to pay. As the Church gathers her strength and becomes a force in the world there is always a backlash.

To date the majority of us have only experienced occasional

mocking. Others have experienced a form of persecution from their own brothers in Christ over one matter or another. But as the Church grows and society begins to be affected by the power of the gospel, real persecution will ensue.

I recently had to fill in an insurance form where I was asked to state my occupation. I wrote, "Christian minister" and was then faced with the question, "Are there any special dangers attached to your job?" I felt like answering, "Not yet!" The man in the street might well scoff at the notion of a minister of religion being engaged in a dangerous occupation, but imagine the apostle Paul filling in the same form! What a catalogue of beatings, imprisonments, shipwrecks and attempted murders he would have to record. We must never forget that we follow a leader who was crucified! When the Church arises in power, threatening world forces and challenging the darkness, a backlash will occur. The battle will require faith and courage. Let us recognise this now and become that army of faith.

An obedient army

The next thing about this army is that it was an obedient army, which was clearly demonstrated by their willingness to follow their leader. The old hymn tells us:

> "Trust and obey
> For there's no other way
> To be happy in Jesus
> Than to trust and obey."[1]

Few would question the importance of obedience in the Christian walk. At the same time we evangelicals have strongly emphasised the *personal* nature of our faith, therefore providing plenty of scope for the individual to actually be independent, wayward and even self-willed. These soldiers demonstrated their obedience to God by obeying their God-given leader.

One might argue that obedience would be easy if our leaders were always like David or Daniel. They were obviously valiant, faithful leaders. But what about Gideon? Following this weak, unremarkable man from the smallest of the tribes must have presented quite a challenge! Yet the Lord chose Gideon, put His Spirit on him and appointed him to lead. By obeying the one whom God has chosen, called and anointed, this army was obeying God. This pinpoints one of the great truths that God is restoring to His Church in these days: leaders must be free to lead.

For too long the Church has been weakened by individualism. Many could sing along with Frank Sinatra, "I did it my way ... " Adam could have sung this as he walked out of the garden. So could Saul as he lost the kingdom. Sin is rooted in "doing it our way". Isaiah tells us that, "Each of us has turned his own way; but the Lord has caused the iniquity of us to fall on Him." We charismatics are particularly vulnerable because we now claim to receive "revelations". We say, "The Lord told me ... " and this can often be independence masquerading as spirituality. Such practice will bring us onto dangerous ground unless we build in the safeguards that are provided by godly leadership which Christ has ordained for His Church. It is certain that we can all hear personally from God – this is an integral part of our inheritance as Christians – but God has also seen our need for mature oversight in the Church.

Many years ago my wife and I borrowed a washing machine and the instructions said, "Before use, secure this to the ground." Since we were only borrowing it temporarily we did not bother. We filled it, turned it on and it chased us around the kitchen! Undisciplined power can create havoc! For some forty years now, God has graciously been pouring out His Spirit on thirsty people. Now He is looking for His army to rise. This means learning the lesson of manifest obedience, not just, "the Lord and me".

Subdivided for action

Gideon divided his men into three groups. No one is recorded as saying, "But I liked it when we were all one." Gideon said, "We are going to be in three sections from now on." He did not invite a vote about it and there is no record that he asked the soldiers what group they wanted to be in. We must take note of this, particularly as God is leading many to divide their churches into congregations, cells and home groups. At such times we find whether or not we have the qualities of this army. Will we go where we are asked to go or reply, "I don't like that group. I would rather be with this one." Some might have been tempted to say, "I want to be with you Gideon. You are the man of God." But God often puts us into situations not just for our immediate blessing, but also for our long-term training.

Joseph was in a lovely "home group" in the beginning – his father's. Then he found himself moved into Potiphar's "house group" and he blessed the house. Wherever he went there was blessing. Then he was transferred from Potiphar's house group to the "prison group" and he blessed the prison! In the end he was such a blessing in the prison that he was given more responsibility. He finally finished up with a group of his own – and quite a large one at that!

Those of you who are jostling for position, are you willing to abandon your personal preferences and say, "Lord, I will stay here and learn from You through this situation. I believe You are teaching me Your ways"?

Jesus often trained His disciples in this kind of way. He asked them to do things that seemed foolish such as casting the net on the other side of the boat. They had been fishing all night, but Jesus said, "Fish on the other side" and they did. At Cana, when they ran out of wine He said, "Go and fill the jars with water" and they did. When they had to pay taxes Jesus said, "Go and catch a fish – you will find a coin there."

What was He doing? He was training this little group to do whatever He said, unswervingly and without question. Gradually He fashioned these men. He sent them on all kinds of peculiar errands which in themselves had no great significance, except that He was teaching them to do these things simply because He said so.

If we are to become an army that will turn the world upside down we have to learn these same lessons. A leader does not want to have to explain his every decision or forever have to coax his people to embrace the vision that God has shown him. Gideon said, "Watch me and what I do, then do likewise." This is one of the hallmarks of anointed leadership. It was not simply a matter of getting others to do things for him; it was instead that Gideon led by example.

Another sign of an authentic leader is that God blesses his activities. If, when Jesus had given His commands, the water had not turned to wine or there had not been a coin in the mouth of the fish, then His followers would have really needed to ask some questions. Real leaders (even though they may sometimes get things wrong) are not forever leading us on ventures that do not work or up blind alleys. If they do, we can question their calling to leadership. On the contrary, with a real leader you can sense that God is with him and you want to be in his slipstream just to see what God will do next.

Can I ask you – do you recognise yourself in this army yet? Are you in a position where a God-given leader can count on your commitment? Have you said to anybody, "I want to join you. I feel that God has raised you up, given you leadership ability and I want to be committed here"? are you with leadership that knows where it's going or are you in a situation that is going nowhere?

All around us sinners are "sitting in darkness and the shadow of death" while the Church remains ineffective. Thousands are dying daily without Christ while the Church goes round in ineffectual circles. May God help us to prepare ourselves for action and find our place in His army – an army with faith, courage and discipline!

Note _____

1. Words: John Sammis, 1887. Music: Daniel Towner, 1887.

CHAPTER 14

Using the Right Weapons

How did this extraordinary army transform apparent defeat into total victory? By using powerful weapons! Yet the weapons they employed were non-material and totally spiritual. Although they were instructed to shout, *"A sword for the LORD and for Gideon"* (Judges 7:20), they did not have one sword between them! They went out with pitchers and lights and trumpets, but no swords. *"The weapons of our warfare,"* Paul wrote, *"are not of the flesh, but divinely powerful"* (2 Corinthians 10:4).

The first significant weapon they used in battle can easily be overlooked. It was, in fact, their *unity*. You might expect me to interpret the spiritual significance of the pitchers, lights and trumpets – they had to break their pitchers and let their lights shine. We might argue, "Isn't the lesson all about breaking the outer man to let God's light shine through?" but personally, I do not believe that this is the heart of the matter at all. Imagine if one individual had embraced the truth regarding the need for "brokenness", had broken his vessel, held up his light and blown his trumpet on his own. The result would have been total failure. The weapons had no value in themselves at all! The power of their strategy was unity – this was their spiritual weapon – they all acted as one man! Without united action these weapons would never work: the spiritual weapon they used was unity. There would have been a total disaster if they had not been absolutely and entirely together in what they were doing.

We must all be committed and loyal to one another for where there is unity God will command blessing. It is easy to feel loyal and united at large Christian conventions where we come and worship together. People embrace, laugh, enjoy good fellowship and sing. In this lovely setting we feel a tremendous sense of oneness. But real unity is seldom tested at these gatherings. The tests start when we have all gone our separate ways. Real unity is challenged when we begin to hear rumours about one another.

Rumours breed fears and anxieties which become suspicions that take form and are then passed on as fact. Gradually, a catalogue of hurt, mistrust and bitterness is inflicted on God's people. True unity, however, develops a heart attitude that will refuse to believe rumours without checking them. Where there is unity rumours will not even be allowed to colour our thinking towards a brother. Christians should not even accept unproven rumours concerning their enemies! How much more then should they be diligent to work out brotherly loyalty to their fellow believers. Rumour and hearsay are to be totally rejected by the people of God.

I wonder if you have ever been to a party where everyone sits in a circle and someone whispers a message in the ear of their neighbour who in turn whispers to the next until the message arrives at the end of the circle. Usually the end message bears no resemblance to the original one. Imagine Gideon's group of three hundred encircling the valley containing the Midianites . . .

The darkness of the night separates them from one another

as they take up their positions. A tiny army of three hundred looks down on the hordes of Midianites. After what seems like an endless delay, waiting for the cry of command, one calls out to his nearest neighbour through the darkness, "What was it we had to shout?"

"A sword for the Lord and Gideon!" comes the reply. "Pass it on."

The next enquires, "What was the cry?"

"Something about Gideon's sword," comes the answer.

After a few more exchanges the message becomes, "Gideon has a sword," until suddenly one frightened and disgruntled soldier sees a terrible injustice here.

"Did you say that Gideon has a sword? Why haven't I got a sword? Gideon has certainly looked after himself, hasn't he? All we have is a light, a pitcher and a trumpet, and Gideon has a sword...!"

It's a farcical scene, but things that are not unlike this happen in the Church of God. Rumours are often not checked out, suspicions are passed on as fact and chaos often prevails. We must fear God and be steadfast and loyal to our brothers. I may be labouring the point, but lack of unity is frustrating the work of God! It has been for years! Will you refuse to accept rumours until you have checked them out and know the truth of the matter? Gideon's men remained united even under pressure; even separated in the darkness!

Paul called the Colossians to put on a heart of compassion, kindness, humility, gentleness and patience, to bear with one another and to forgive just as they had been forgiven. He reminded them that God had commanded His chosen people to put on love, which is the perfect bond of unity, and to let Christ rule in their hearts. If we forget that we are members of one another we will never be united and without unity we will never become an effective army.

Having strategy

The second powerful spiritual weapon deployed at the battle of Gideon was divine strategy. Each one stood in his place. The ruse required was that these men should give the appearance of a vast army. They had to be properly staggered around the hillside. Each light, each trumpet and each shout had to make a contribution by virtue of their being in exactly the right place.

Imagine Gideon's soldiers finding their places around the hillside. One sees an elderly lady struggling with a heavy load of provisions and offers her help. Another hears a little boy lost in a cave and goes to find him. These distractions, however worthy in themselves, would have been in total conflict with God's strategy for that moment. It would have cost them the battle.

Is your light shining where God wants it to? He wants us in the place of maximum impact. We are not meant to be stumbling upon random "good causes". Each of us has significance in our own right and is ultimately going to give an account of what we have done with our light. We are not driftwood; we are meant to be standing in the best possible place to count for God.

Playing your part

Thirdly, Gideon's soldiers were not only standing in the right place, they were all fully functioning and actively involved with torches, pitchers and trumpets. There was no chance for inactivity!

Ephesians 4 tells us that we shall come to fullness of stature when every part is working properly. Gideon's army would have been destroyed if someone had been missing. Imagine the chaos if one shouted and then another while others grouped together to shine their lights. We must all be in our places and working properly, then the impact will be enormous.

The great contrast between Gideon's army and the Church today is that each member had identical tasks, whereas the Church displays infinite variety. God has blessed us with such a variety of gifts that, added together, make the Church wonderful and glorious. Consider for a moment the diversity and spectacular beauty of the creation. Wildlife programmes on television often give us unparalleled glimpses of multicoloured flora and fauna, of forests, mountains, lakes and seas. We see infinite variety. God has not even made two snowflakes alike and yet, incredibly, all creation is going to be wrapped up as a garment and thrown away. But His Church will live forever! His glorious Church with all its variety is the pinnacle of God's creative skill. Is it right that we should go to church on Sundays just to sing four hymns, hear a sermon and then go home? What a waste of all God's wonderful gifts. Remember, only the Church survives – the rest of creation will be cast away. The seas, mountains and forests have not captivated Him – however much they impress us – but the beautiful, wonderful, multicoloured Church, God will keep forever.

I remember an elderly man in a church that I used to visit occasionally. One day I asked him how he was and for a quarter of an hour he poured out his sorrows. On my next visit I forgot my previous experience and recklessly asked him again! He repeated his tale of woe. Amazingly, it happened a third time. On this occasion I felt that I had to speak, reminding him that for the believer life was anything but negative. Months later I visited the church again and noticed my friend looking very different. He told me that God had given him a little ministry. It transpired that he had been obtaining old birthday cards, inserting fresh inside pages and then, in beautiful copperplate handwriting, had filled them with scriptures and poems. He had sent these out to the lonely and the elderly – to anybody he heard was in need. He then showed me letters of gratitude that he had received from many who had been helped by his unusual but helpful ministry.

When Paul lists his gifts of the Spirit I do not remember one entitled, "writing poems in old birthday cards," but there are such a variety of ways in which we can encourage one another that not one of us needs to remain unfulfilled. This man's life was transformed as he found a lovely ministry that was appropriate for him at his stage in life. God wants every one of us in the right place, working fully and effectively in His glorious Church.

Cast on God

Finally, Gideon's army was not only characterised by its unity and its use of spiritual weapons, but also by tactics that were totally dependent on God. They did not adopt the attitude that they had to do everything themselves, nor did they passively say, "It's all God's work – we are 'letting go and letting God'. We just hand it over to Him and He will do it."

The battle of Midian reveals a beautiful balance of human responsibility and divine intervention. We must not be passively waiting for angelic activity. We must seek God for strategy. Amazingly, we are co-workers with God and we fellowship with Him in the work! Although God could triumph without us He invites us to be involved in His plan. He has different strategies for different battles. The strategy for taking Jericho was to walk round it and shout. The strategy for Ai was to set up an ambush. So, we must not assume that because a certain method worked on one occasion that this must be the accepted pattern from now on! God will not be locked into a formula or method. He wants to share His plans with us so that we get to know Him.

Gideon's army was united. Each member was in the right place at the right time and functioning properly. They had a strategy but they were still totally dependent on God. In this context He was able to move. The Midianites did not flee just because of some noise and a few moments of confusion. They fled because God set the sword of each one against another throughout the army. Gideon's manoeuvres, no matter how skilfully accomplished, could not destroy an army. God stepped in!

We must continually seek God for His strategy in our generation and then ask for His powerful presence to transform our endeavours into God-like proportions.

Gideon's victory was total. The Midianites were devastated and fled. With great rejoicing they pursued their enemies and totally defeated them with a memorable victory.

A last word

To conclude we must see one final lesson from this battle. Gideon invited all the men of Ephraim to become involved in the defeat of Midian. There was no attempt to claim the victory exclusively for his handpicked three hundred. Gideon wanted to involve the whole nation. When some men of Ephraim challenged him with exclusiveness he was quick to disarm them with his openheartedness: he drew them in. It was not in his heart to lead a small, separate, elitist group. He had seen God move with power and there had been a great victory; Gideon wanted to share this with *all* of the Lord's people.

There is no room for any to claim special status in the conflict we face today. God is for all His people so we must learn to be like Him and welcome one another in the love of Christ.

We began by noting that Isaiah 9 promises the ever-increasing government of Christ and likens its advance to the battle of Midian. To thoroughly conquer Midian and see Christ's kingdom win we must all unite and take to the battlefield together. Past misunderstandings, divisions and hurts must be put away. If God's kingdom is to be established, forgiveness must prevail. Forgetting what is behind we must press on, reaching forward to what lies ahead. May God enable us to learn the lessons and fulfil God's purpose in our generation.

PART 3

Nehemiah

*"The God of heaven will give us success;
therefore we His servants will arise and build . . . "*
(Nehemiah 2:20)

Blessed Are Those Who Mourn

15

There was a day in the life of Nehemiah that started like any other, but by the end of it he was a changed man. The motivation for his life and his expectations concerning his career were transformed.

God can do this for you as you read this book. He could come to you and turn your life upside down. You may have thought, "I have my career, I know my path in life," but God could come and speak to you in such a way as to make your career insignificant. You could discover, like Nehemiah, "From now on Zion is my chief delight. From now on to see the city rebuilt, to see the Church of God restored from ruins is the top priority in my life." It could happen in one day. It can happen when listening to just one sermon.

One day Moses was with the same sheep, doing the same routine, when he saw the bush burning! His life was never the same again! The day had started like any other day, but a burning bush made all the difference.

One day David was looking after a few of his father's sheep when one of his brothers came rushing up the hill, gasping as he gave him a message: " David, Samuel is here. He wants to see you!" David hurried off to his memorable encounter with Samuel and his life was never the same again!

One day Isaiah was in the house of God. Israel's great king had died and Isaiah faced the future with concern when suddenly he saw the Lord, high and lifted up. In a moment his life was revolutionised.

Gideon, frightened little Gideon, was hiding away. Suddenly an angel of the Lord spoke to him. This was his turning point.

Paul, breathing out threats and slaughter against the Church, suddenly saw a light!

One day the God-fearing Nehemiah in his safe, secure job simply heard some news – but it changed his life completely. The whole course of his life was transformed in one day. What news did he hear? "The wall of Jerusalem is broken down and its gates are burned with fire."

Years earlier, pioneers had returned from captivity in Babylon to rebuild Jerusalem from its ruins. The city of God had been desecrated, but Nehemiah thought that the rebuilding was already under way. Instead, Zion was a pathetic heap of rubble. The walls were down and anybody could walk in; the gates were burned; they were in "great distress, shame and reproach." Nehemiah was overwhelmed with the news. He was devastated.

Take heed how you hear

As I reflected on this it occurred to me how we can be very bad hearers of news. Jesus said, "Take heed how you hear." In today's world we have so much information coming at us from television, the Internet, radio and newspapers, that devastating news can be heard so passively, so indifferently; we can be so preoccupied.

For instance, we can see news about a drought in Africa and be deeply moved for a moment as we see tiny children and their emaciated bodies. The news is starkly real and our hearts go out to them. But then there is the next item of news, followed by another and another, and eventually, as is so often the case, the news comes to a conclusion with something utterly trivial. We go on to watch the next programme, forgetting the plight in Africa or the earthquake in Pakistan.

We hear news all the time, but we do not know *how* to hear it. "Take heed *how* you hear." We can be moved for a moment and yet not have heard enough to change us. However, Nehemiah heard and this was all it took. He was devastated. Oh, that we might be so sensitive!

You may be driving along the motorway listening to the radio. You hear one tune after another and you may even hear an appeal for a charity and be moved for a moment. But there is another way of listening. Suddenly the announcer interrupts the show with a news flash about an accident, naming a person or place. If you are related to the person or have family or friends in that certain place you hear this news differently! You are gripped. You stop and try to make contact.

This is how we need to hear. Jesus said, *"For the heart of this people has become dull, with their ears they scarcely hear..."* (Matthew 13:15). Listen to these words of Jesus:

> *"Then He will say to those on His left, 'Depart from Me, accursed ones, into the eternal fire which has been prepared for the devil and his angels ... these will go away into eternal punishment, but the righteous into eternal life."*
>
> (Matthew 25:41, 46)

How well did you hear? It is true that we have become dull of hearing – we find it very difficult to hear, *"they will go away into eternal punishment."*

Jesus said, "Take heed how you hear. This people's hearts have become dull, their ears barely hear." But God says from heaven, "This is My beloved Son – *hear Him*. He understands about life and death. He understands about eternity. He dwelt in eternity with me. He knows and can speak with authority about eternal matters. Beloved, *hear Him*. He is My dear Son." Have we heard the news? Has it gripped us? Has it devastated us?

A glorious Church

Hear another piece of news. Jesus wants a spotless, perfect Bride, *"fair as the moon, clear as the sun, and terrible as an army of banners"* (Song of Songs 6:10 AV). This is what He wants. This is what He is going to have. When we consider how glorious Zion is meant to be, are we overwhelmed by the thought and the vision? It can only happen when we realise that God has declared that Christ died for a glorious Church.

We need to be overwhelmed before we can become useful to God. We need to look at the situation of the Church today and we need to look at our society where the walls that say, "This is acceptable and this is not acceptable," are down. In the very beginning God separated light and darkness, and ever since then He has been in the business of separating and dividing. So it is a great tragedy when the walls of society crumble.

Without any doubt the walls are coming down. Our nations are afflicted with the scourge of AIDS and other diseases that owe their origin to promiscuity. Yet the cry is not, "How can we stop promiscuity?" but rather, "How can we cure AIDS?"

The real tragedy is when the walls come down in church life. The newspapers are reporting that ministers are giving blessings to gay marriages. Where is the wall that says, "No, this is not acceptable within the Church of God"?

Let me show you what the world thinks of the Church. A national newspaper carried an article by a political journalist –

not a religious columnist – a political expert, under the heading, "You can't sell faith like cornflakes". He said this about the Church:

> "Over the past generation a process of demoralization has set in among the clergy. Watching their flocks diminish, they have tended to hold less strongly to their own convictions or, rather, they have found secular substitutes for a dogmatic religious faith which is waning. In place of the Christianity of the Ten Commandments they have put their Christianity of social welfare. They concern themselves with what they imagine are burning topical issues, they hold debates on nuclear weapons, some of them campaign actively on behalf of pacifist bodies, preach sermons on unemployment. Sometimes they behave as though they were little more than social workers. Sometimes they try to usurp the functions of government ministers. They are almost invariably well-meaning, progressive-minded, humanitarian and, to use the current catchphrase, caring and compassionate. But there is nothing more to distinguish these high-minded bishops, deans, canons and reverends from any other category of do-gooders. The charismatic element seems to have gone. They are manifestly not divinely inspired. There is not much faith in their hearts or fire in their bellies, and it shows! It seems to me that there is absolutely no future for the Church as a social welfare institution. At the same time, the Church has watered down its teaching on almost all aspects of morality. If young people seek guidance on sexual conduct, for instance, they are no longer offered definite rules, but are given polysyllabic fudge and mush. People turn to God not in order to seek their own materialist, earthly desires, but to escape from them.

The Church is meant to offer something which is better and ennobling. Religion is not about this world – it is about the next. Christianity is not a secular crusade for social improvements – it is an alternative to materialism. A rejection of the world and the flesh, it concentrates instead on the eternal and the divine. The notion that it can be democratized and popularized is nonsense. It operates on the frontiers of human understanding and makes heroic demands of its adherents. That indeed is precisely its appeal: because it is so totally and constitutionally different from anything else to be found in the world. Of course, to preach this kind of Christianity – the only true kind – requires a passionate faith which is very uncharacteristic of many churchmen. Preferring to operate with the techniques of modern religious sociology they are in fact getting absolutely nowhere."

This journalist's article does not conclude with biblical answers, but he is able to discern the shambles. He is saying, "Look, they are being compassionate and caring like any other do-gooders, but where is their distinctive message? Are they not supposed to be distinctive and different?" He concludes that the whole thing is humbug. The photograph with the article is a communion service being held at Centre Court, Wimbledon! The world says, "Nonsense! We are not impressed!"

The world regards the Church as irrelevant to modern living. We need to hear this news. The walls are down and the world can see it! The gates are not there – anybody can walk in and say anything. And this is where the story begins; when people, young men and women, older people like Nehemiah, hear this news in such a way that it triggers something off within them and they cry, "Enough! We cannot stand this any longer." God has said that His city will be the joy of the whole earth and the world says that it is humbug! This realisation must come to us with such force that we cannot stand still any longer. The shame should hit us hard.

Nehemiah felt that igniting spark trigger something deep within his spirit. Has it happened to you yet? Has Zion become the chief motivation in your life? You may be a school teacher, a nurse or a banker, but can you truly say that the kingdom of God comes first. Everything else has to take second place. For some of us this is going to mean that we can no longer be a teacher, a nurse or a banker. We will find that we must give our lives to rebuilding the city of God.

Weeping first, working later

First of all, Nehemiah heard the news. Secondly, he cried to God. In his need Nehemiah wept, mourned, fasted and prayed. His first response was not action. If our first response is action we betray the fact that we have failed to see the enormity of the problem. We simply have not understood. The situation has not overwhelmed us. We have not sat and down and wept. To think we can just put on a crusade and change things is like administering aspirin to someone with terminal cancer. It is a hopeless endeavour. We have to fall down, mourn and pray.

Some of us are at ease because we have the biggest church in town. But what is two to three thousand people in a town of thirty thousand? What is one thousand in an urban area of three hundred thousand? Our churches may have become the largest in town, but what is that against the vast crowds who do not know that Jesus is alive and think that the Church is a joke? We must allow this to hurt us. It must penetrate us to the core. When Nehemiah considered the reality it overwhelmed him!

Until we have wept over the ruins we will never build the wall. If we have begun to see scores of people crowding into

our churches and have been tempted to think that we have hit
the jackpot we should go from door to door where five
thousand people live on a local housing estate and ask them
how interested they are in Jesus. When the reality overwhelms
us we shall start crying to God. The Bible does not say, "Have a
go." It does not say, "Blessed are the whiz kids who know how
to get the publicity moving" or "Blessed are those who know
how to use the media." Instead it says, "Blessed are those who
know how to mourn." Why? Because they shall be *fortified*.
"Fortified" is a better translation than "comforted". When
the Bible was first translated into English, "comfort" carried the
meaning that "fortify" has retained today. When we think
about comfort we think about cushions and armchairs, but
when the Bible says, "Blessed are those who mourn, for they
shall be comforted" and "I will send the Comforter" it means
something more than ease and rest.

Our basic understanding of the Holy Spirit's ministry has
been affected by the way this English word has changed its
meaning. When Wycliffe first penned the word it meant, "to
fortify, strengthen, provoke or stir up". Today it carries more of
a "there, there" meaning. Our hymnbooks often reflect this
with their gentle hymns about the Holy Spirit: "There, there,
don't worry – the Holy Spirit will comfort." No! The word is
"fortify"!

I believe that Nehemiah grieved, red-eyed in the dust, crying
out, "Lord, this is so disgraceful, so shameful, that Your city
should come to this!" Such a heartfelt response is an alien
concept to many who call themselves evangelical. But so often
we are coldly evangelical, withstanding-the-Holy-Ghost evangelical! We stand on our traditions and claim we are true to the
Bible, but still say "No" to the Holy Spirit. In repentance we
must admit, "Oh God, it is shameful that Your house is in
ruins."

When we humbly begin to agree with God He can begin to fortify us: "Blessed are those who mourn, for they shall be fortified."

Nehemiah was first of all overwhelmed by the reality. It consumed him. His chief thought was, "The city of God is in ruins." We too must be gripped by the enormity of the problem so that God can begin to fortify us. Nehemiah turned to God as his only answer. God is our only answer too – not trying special meetings, not endeavouring to manipulate the media. We need God! It is as basic as this! After his mourning Nehemiah was transformed, fortified, commissioned! From that time on no obstacle thrown across his path could stop him!

16

Passion for Zion

When Nehemiah began to pray, his prayer was one of the most memorable and instructive prayers in the Bible. First of all he cried out to the *God of heaven*. When we see our own puny endeavours we can be so grateful that our God is the God of the heaven, the eternal God, the glorious God. Great and marvellous, He rides on the heavens to our help. It is when we see the enormity of our problems that we are absolutely cast on Him – not to bless our puny ideas, but to take over. The God of the heavens is our only hope. We need heaven's power, heaven's resources and heaven's conviction. We need God to move in convicting power to bring about revival. I was deeply stirred when I read about J.O. Fraser's experiences in China as recorded in *Mountain Rain*.[1] He made prayer his major occupation and, after several years, hundreds of families in many villages were swept into the kingdom.

The great and terrible God

When Nehemiah cried out to "the God of the heavens", he addressed Him as "the great and terrible God". Nehemiah was not fooled into thinking that God had diminished in power because the nation was in need and the city was in ruins. He still believed that He was the great and terrible God. He is great and terrible – so much bigger than our subjective view of Him. This is why it is so edifying to sing great truths about God that come straight from the pages of Scripture rather than derive our doctrine of God from sentimental songs and hymns.

When we read of Zechariah, for instance, we probably think of him as a prophet of encouragement – and he certainly was – but the very first word that Zechariah prophesied was the word "angry". Zechariah 1:2 reads, *"The LORD was very angry with your fathers."* It was because God was angry that He sent His people into humiliating captivity in Babylon. We have such a plastic view of God that we tend to forget the He can be angry. When they returned to Jerusalem as a "restoration people" they still failed to build and Zechariah had to say to them, "Listen, God was angry with your fathers. Do not think, just because you have come back and have experienced some of God's blessing that you can drift along. No! God has not changed. He still requires wholehearted commitment to His purposes." He is still the great and terrible God. It is a fearful thing to fall into the hands of the living God and we must never forget it.

Moving from that foundation, Nehemiah began to reckon on another great truth. He addressed God as the One "who keeps His covenant of love with those who love Him and keep His commandments". Although He is angry, although He is great and terrible, He is also the God of covenant love with His people. He has made a covenant with His chosen and He has determined a future for them. Let us take note as we see how Nehemiah pressed on in intercession: "Father, I know You are great, I know You are awesome, I know You are terrible, but Lord, we are Your people and You have made a covenant." If we are to be effective intercessors it is vital to be persuaded that we come to a God of covenant love. We can pray, "Lord, You made a covenant with us in Your dear Son. We may be weak at present, but You are for us, You are with us!"

We can begin to argue our case. Prayer is arguing your case. Look at the greatest pray-ers in the Bible – they are arguing the case: "Lord, if this is so, what about this?" Abraham is a good example. He argues, "Lord, if there are this many righteous will You save the city? Lord, if there are *this* many . . . ?"

Look at Moses. He said, "God, if I have found favour, if I have found grace, show me Your glory" – arguing from one thing to the next. Do you argue your case before God? We need to pray, "Lord You have promised," so that we plead the promises as our way to receive mighty answers. He is a covenant-keeping God with whom we may dare to argue.

Nehemiah said, *"Remember the word which You commanded your servant Moses"* (Nehemiah 1:8). This is the way to pray: "Lord, *You* said it. It is not *our* idea." This is why Elijah prayed that the rain would stop. It was not just Elijah's bright idea. He did not think, "What shall I pray to impress people? I know, I will pray that the rain will stop." He did not suddenly have a brainwave. He knew that Deuteronomy said, "If you go after false gods I will shut the heavens, I will stop the rain" (see Deuteronomy 11:17). He knew what God had promised and how to argue those promises with God.

Nehemiah was not going to experiment with his own schemes. He was cast on God: "God, You promised. I am pleading the case before You now!" Moving on, we see that Nehemiah also identified with the sin of the nation. He said, *"We* have sinned!" We need to identify. We need to say, "Oh God, we are part of this Church that is a laughing stock." We would like to stand back from it and not be associated with something that is seen as a weak, irrelevant anachronism, but we are part of the whole. As we acknowledge our common identity as children of God we will feel the weight of responsibility and become strongly motivated intercessors.

Next Nehemiah reminded God, "Lord Your Word says that if we turn against You, You will scatter us; but if we turn to You, You will gather us again to the place that You have chosen to cause Your name to dwell." It is interesting to note that in God's purpose scattering represents judgement and gathering is part of the blessing. God is gathering a people in these days. Have you been gathered, as it says here, "to a place where He is causing His name to dwell"? Gathering is part of God's mercy in renewal so that He can manifest His name and glory.

Then Nehemiah used this last argument. He said, "They are *Your* people." I underlined my Bible at all the places where it says "Your" in Nehemiah 1:10: *"They are Your servants and Your people whom You redeemed by Your great strength and by Your strong hand"* (emphasis added). Nehemiah threw the whole onus back onto God. He said, "Lord, these are Your people. There is an awful mess, but they are Yours, Lord."

Moses used the same method when he argued, "Lord, they are Your people. What will the heathen say? That You are not able to bring them into the land?" Jesus did the same thing in John 17: "Yours they were and You gave them to Me. Now, Lord, I am committing them to You. They are Yours, Lord. Your name is attached to them."

We must bring this argument to God when we say, "Oh God, we are Your beloved people, Your Church, Your great name is involved!" Do you travail with God like this? God is looking for people who will. We are so casual. God is looking for people who will come before Him and plead His Church and His great name – "Blessed are those who mourn, for they shall be fortified!"

Nehemiah commissioned

The opening chapter shows Nehemiah as a broken-hearted man, but after his encounter with God he never looked back. He started weeping, fasting and crying, but after this chapter it did not matter what problems he encountered – absolutely nothing was going to stop him. Talk about a fortified man! He was marvellous! He leaps out from the pages – a wonderful three-dimensional figure! Why? Because God fortified him. God strengthened him. God came to him in his mourning.

Do you mourn in your poverty stricken spirit? You are really blessed. Why? Because you refuse to depend on your own resources. If you are poor in spirit you are in a position to receive grace, so don't despair; say instead, "Thank You Lord. The situation is overwhelming but You can fortify me."

Ex-cupbearer

At the very end of the first chapter Nehemiah added one important detail: "Now I was cupbearer to the king." The highly significant role as cupbearer to the king no longer held any real importance – he didn't use this privileged rank to impress his readers, he merely mentioned it at the end. His priorities were established.

We do not know about God's secret dealings with Nehemiah. What we would term "Nehemiah's call" is not recorded for us, but during those days with God, those days of prayer, clearly God began to deal with him. After his encounter with God he could say to the king, "Send me to Judah, to the city of my fathers' tombs." This phrase, "the city of my fathers' tombs" really caught my attention. He had a sense of history. He wanted to go back to the city where his fathers were. He was gripped by the honour of his family.

You might well argue that this does not apply to you. You are the only one in your family who is converted to Christ. You do not come from a Christian background. No, you are thinking about the wrong family. Once you are born again you belong to another family altogether. Zion is the city of your family and your fathers' tombs. There are amazing tombs in Zion – did you know this? Tombs of great men and women down through the ages. You have joined a wonderful family. Wesley was in it; Whitefield was in it.

I have recently been reading about some of the great reformers; men who laid down their lives, like Tyndale who translated the Scriptures. Such men are our fathers. Their tombs are there. Reading again, after many years, J.C. Ryle's book, *Five Great Reformers*, I met once more Bishop Hooper as he laid down his life in the flames. A reformer to the end, he prevailed for the truth, even though it meant being condemned to the stake. Three times they had to light the firewood around his legs. The first time it blazed up, burnt his arm and went out! After they had lit the flames again the wind changed direction, but this man stood bound to the stake saying wonderful, glorious things about his Saviour.

These heroes are part of our family! They have gone before us in order to give us the Scriptures, in order to see the Church of God come to fullness. We need to say, "Let me see the city of my fathers' tombs again. I want to see a city that is worthy of their sacrifice. I want to see a Church that speaks of the glory of these men who laid down their lives."

I will rebuild it

Nehemiah said, "Send me to Judah, to the city of my fathers' tombs that I may rebuild it." He was so stirred up by the challenge that he said, "I am going to rebuild it," almost implying that even if no one else went, he was still going to. How foreign this is to the thinking that says, *"Someone* ought to do *something* about it. We will draw up a committee." The men who got things done never thought like this. Even if the whole scheme looked totally impossible they would still say, "I am going to build it!" These are the men and women who change situations, who find, once they start building, that there is a whole army to help them. They do not say, *"Someone* ought to do something"; they themselves seek God until He ignites a fire in their hearts and then cry, "Let me get to it; let me see Your Church restored!"

Don't you long for the day when in every town, in every place, there is a glorious testimony – hundreds of worshipping, praising people? Every year we gather thousands of teenagers to our "Newday" conference. As we praise and worship God every day the staff are always amazed to see so many young people excited about God. They have commented, "It's a pity the Church isn't like this!" How true this is! The world has no time for empty religion; it has no time for arguing about whether we should raise our hands in meetings. They are bewildered that the Church majors on such trivialities. They don't mind us taking over their showground and making a lot of noise; they are used to people making noise. Christians have this strange preoccupation with little things: "We have always done it this way . . ."

We claim to have the answer to the world's needs. Many of us claim to be scrupulously evangelical and are horrified at hearing the news of gay marriages being blessed in churches. But still we are preoccupied with the trifle of our churches' traditional minutiae. Meanwhile, the world regards us as irrelevant and who can blame them?

When the world sees reality they will be open-mouthed. They will say, "We didn't know that the Church was like this!"

They will throng to see it. Amazed by it, they will look forward to us coming. If we are obedient we shall see more and more blessing. It will be tough, as we shall see through chapter after chapter of Nehemiah's experience. A hornet's nest will be stirred up when we, like Nehemiah, have the welfare of God's people as our first love rather than the status quo.

We have to be possessed with the same passion as our fathers before us. It is hopeless to settle for the current situation saying, "We have our traditions here." They had their traditions when they burned Hooper at the stake and when Tyndale was hounded to his death. This is why they killed them! Where is the spirit of the reformers? Where are the people who will say, "Persecute me if you will, but I am going to rebuild the house of God!" We have got to have this brand of passion. It may seem impossible, but Nehemiah boldly affirmed, "I am going to rebuild. I am going to do something about it!"

Note

1. Eileen Crossman, *Mountain Rain*, Authentic Lifestyle, 1984.

It Was Very Displeasing to Them

17

How suddenly Nehemiah's life was changed! His established routine was transformed by what he heard and he became a man of destiny.

A young pastor once attended one of our conferences for ministers. He had been developing his church in a fairly traditional way and then suddenly, he one day heard about God's purpose to restore the Church. "Now I am ruined," he said, "I cannot settle for anything less."

Nehemiah became a man gripped by a vision. His burden was to see Zion restored, her walls standing, her gates strong and firm and the purposes of God established. But fulfilling that vision involved a battle. Powerful enemies opposed Nehemiah:

> *"When Sanballat . . . and Tobiah . . . heard about it, it was very displeasing to them that someone had come to seek the welfare of the sons of Israel."*
>
> (Nehemiah 2:10)

As you read on you will find that this concern quickly developed into fury and anger (see Nehemiah 4:1). We have a spiritual enemy, the devil, who is furious that the Church is being restored. He has been so happy to see its disarray, lacking in faith and a sense of destiny. To see the Church beginning to gain fresh impetus – to see Christians arise like Nehemiah, purposing to rebuild – brings trembling and fear, anger and fury into the enemy camp. He therefore provokes conflict. It has not been easy to restore the Church. Bruised and battered, we have come through many crises as the spiritual battle rages.

As we consider the story of Nehemiah we find the devil trying many different schemes to prevent the rebuilding of the city. We also discover many amazing parallels with our contemporary scene. The devil tries many disguises. If one trick does not work he switches to another in his hostility toward the Church. Remember, he's not only interested in little old you! He wants to stop the whole city being built and, in as much as you are part of that, he attacks you. Every way he can he will try to stop the rebuilding programme. Throughout the conflict it is vital that we remember that our battle is not against flesh and blood, but against spiritual forces opposed to God.

Mighty mockery

The first weapon the devil chose to use was mockery. They began to laugh:

> "Now it came about that when Sanballat heard that we were rebuilding the wall, he became furious and very angry and mocked the Jews. He spoke in the presence of his brothers and the wealthy men of Samaria and said, 'What are these feeble Jews doing? Are they going to restore it for themselves? Can they offer sacrifices? Can they finish in a day? Can they revive the stones from the dusty rubble even the burned ones?' Now Tobiah the Ammonite was near him and he said, 'Even what they are

> *building – if a fox should jump on it, he would break their stone wall down!'"*
>
> (Nehemiah 4:1–3)

Taken at face value mockery sounds as though it is an expression of indifference, but the Bible reveals what was behind it all. They were not indifferent at all. They were furious and angry and were using mockery as a deliberate weapon.

The devil is very cunning. He knows our flesh. He knows how we hate to be ridiculed. Man naturally wants to be honoured and respected; he wants to be accepted, not laughed at. Many will desert the spiritual battlefield because of the pain inflicted through mockery. If secret pride hides in our hearts mockery will certainly bring it to the surface and uncover our hidden motivations.

Sanballat was not alone either. He poured scorn on the Jews *"before his brothers and the wealthy men of Samaria."* Ridicule from the sophisticated "in crowd" is hard to bear. Those who seem to have "got it together" can use the weapon with devastating force.

Christian women with unconverted husbands often have to endure mockery such as: "Surely you're not going to that silly church again with all those gullible people?" aimed at unsettling their newfound faith. Sometimes, teenagers experience similar comments from unconverted parents: "Don't you realise that modern science has disproved Christianity?" It sounds so casual, but can be so powerful and inflict deep wounds. If we are going to triumph over this enemy of ours we must face up to the fact that the gospel is foolishness to natural man. We are tempted to pray for successful sportsmen and pop singers so that we can have some of our pride back. We often think, "If only a prestigious person could be saved ... we could all stand up and say, 'He's a scientist and he's a Christian.'"

No, the gospel is folly! Natural man thinks it is nonsense that our hopes are built on Jesus of Nazareth who died on a cross in the Middle East two thousand years ago. It is nonsense to modern twenty-first century man. But we must also remember that it was nonsense to the Greeks of Paul's day and that he endured mockery in Athens. Experiencing sarcasm and scorn is part of taking up our cross and following our beloved Lord Jesus, who endured mockery to the end.

Ridicule is not only used to attack the faith of individuals. In Nehemiah's day it was used to oppose the restoration programme. They said, "Even if a fox ran up there the whole thing would collapse!" You can imagine their critics laughing at them.

Twenty-first century attempts at the restoration of the Church have been similarly attacked: "They call themselves a church, but they don't even have a proper clergy or a proper church building! There is no scholarship amongst them! What serious theologian is allied with them? It will all blow over in a few years."

Crippling compromise

Because ridicule and scorn did not stop Nehemiah, his opponents resorted to another approach. They had confidently predicted that nothing would prosper but, "the walls got to half their height and the people had a mind to work." Jerusalem was beginning to take on some stature and a look of permanence. The whole project was taking off with growth and progress all around. So they turned to their next weapon, namely, compromise: "Let us meet together, let us talk about this. Hold on a minute – you're moving at quite a pace. It looks as though it's going to stand after all. We need to have a round table conference." The context shows that their plan was actually to destroy the work of God, but it came under the guise of "having a talk about things". The ugly weapon of compromise!

I look back to when I was a young Christian, longing to be filled with the Holy Spirit. I remember spending a whole evening in my bedroom praying about receiving the Holy Spirit. I was longing to find the answer. At the end of the evening my door opened and my father most lovingly said to me, "Come on son, you mustn't take this religion thing too seriously." Have you heard this sort of thing? Have you heard, "Don't take it too seriously. We don't mind you going to church on Sunday, but you must keep things in proportion. That church of yours is not like other churches – it gets very noisy down there! Why do you take it all so seriously?"

Many face this challenge, especially after God has called them into full-time service or to some other particular step of commitment. We hear such reasonable arguments as, "Be careful. You cannot refuse that promotion – you've been waiting for it for years and you deserve it. Think what it will mean for your income." If the devil cannot laugh us out of court he whispers, "For goodness' sake, don't take it too seriously ... "

This cajoling is so persuasive: "You cannot give up all that. The promotion would give you a very influential position. In your spare time you could still do a lot for the church. Be reasonable!" The call to sweet reason can be a very powerful weapon in the enemy's hand: "God wants you to be reasonable. He doesn't want you to be fanatical." So doubt is sown in our minds: "Am I being fanatical? Perhaps I am being short-sighted. Am I throwing everything away?" The battle rages as the devil tries to destroy the onward purpose of your life and the advance of the restoration of the Church.

I am sure you have met people who ask, "Why must you insist on speaking in tongues and all that noisy worship? Why don't you do that elsewhere and leave us to have our Sunday services as we have always had them? Why don't you show love and keep others happy? If you must have that charismatic meeting you can have it in your own house, but let's keep Sunday decent and in order. A lot of people in the church don't like it. Remember, the Holy Spirit never brings division – the Holy Spirit is always loving."

This kind of reasoning can have crippling power, especially when a recently baptised-in-the-Spirit young preacher has his salary, his home, his wife and children and his whole security to think about. He realises that to be true to his vision might well result in a loss of all material security. Rightly he thinks, "Where shall we live? What shall we do? I suppose I could compromise. Perhaps we could have just a few Scripture songs and perhaps I could ask people not to raise their hands on a Sunday, and we could somehow settle at a level where everybody is happy?"

A pastor recently told me that he had resigned from his local church. He acknowledged, "For too long I tried leading from the middle and you cannot do it." He had been trying to keep everybody happy, but in the end the situation nearly destroyed him.

Nehemiah refused to compromise. He was gripped by a vision to see Zion restored and the walls erected. The apostle Paul was driven by a similar commitment. He saw himself as one called by God and entrusted with the gospel, and therefore made it his aim to speak as one *"not as pleasing men, but God who examines our hearts"* (1 Thessalonians 2:4). Paul knew that his final examination would be before the throne of God and he was more concerned to please his God than to please man. Though at all times he tried to put no stumbling block in the way of others, nothing would prevent his obedience to the vision that God had put before him.

If we are to fulfil our calling and the purpose of God in our generation we shall have to learn to overcome the challenge of mockery and compromise. However, the battle does not end here. Satan has more weapons in his arsenal, as we shall go on to see.

"It Is Reported – You Are to Be Their King"

18

Nehemiah's enemies had not finished just yet. They tried a third powerful weapon. Sanballat sent his servant to Nehemiah with an open letter in which was written,

> *"It is reported among the nations, and Gashmu says, that you and the Jews are planning to rebel; therefore you are rebuilding the wall. And you are to be their king, according to these reports."*

(Nehemiah 6:6)

Here was the next attack: first mockery, then compromise and now flagrant lies! *"It is reported . . . "* What was reported?

"You are starting a rebellion, a takeover – and you are to be the king. And you have also appointed prophets to proclaim concerning you, 'A king is in Judah!' " In other words, Nehemiah was being attacked for setting up an authority structure.

How incredible! This could have been written in the twenty-first century because such misrepresentation is so common today. With a quick addition of "There's no smoke without fire" accusations fly left, right and centre.

Invited by a group of ministers to explain the theology of our church, I happily responded then also pointed out to them that we were not inventing a new theology, but were simply, as evangelicals, trying to be wholeheartedly biblical. I spoke briefly and then suggested that they might like to ask some questions. The rest of our time together was spent in answering these. Towards the end they asked about our "authority structure" within the church. They explained, "We have heard that if anybody in your church wants to redecorate their home or buy new furniture they have to get permission." Turning to one of their members they indicated that he had told them this was the case. Immediately the man denied that he had firsthand knowledge, but had simply "heard it" from someone else. Each one in turn denied that they had been the original source of this rumour.

Happily, I was able to reassure them and say that we were not in the slightest bit interested in directing people concerning their house decorations or furniture!

Amazingly, they then produced another even more incredible story. This time they prefaced their remarks by assuring me that they knew this particular case was true because one of their group had been acquainted with the facts. It seems that they had heard of a couple who wanted to join our church. The wife was acceptable to us but the husband was not, so we had required them to be divorced before she could join. I sat there appalled! I asked which of the men before me could give me more details because I knew nothing at all about it. Incredibly, the same thing that had happened before was repeated – not one of them acknowledged that they actually knew anything about it personally. We paused while they argued, "Surely *you* told us about it, didn't you?" All of them denied being the original source too. My heart was very heavy as I pleaded with them, "Brothers, neither of these things is true and none of you seem to know where the original stories came from."

Nehemiah's opponents also challenged his motivation. They

claimed that he wanted to be king. What a total and tragic fabrication and distortion of the truth! The Bible tells us what Nehemiah's motivation was – he was broken-hearted about the condition of Israel and he longed to see Zion restored. This was his only motivation. He wanted to see Zion changed into a city set on a hill that could not be hidden. He wanted to replace piles of rubbish with clear cut walls and gates. He wanted to see the purpose of God fulfilled in his generation.

Formidable fear

Fear was their next device. Shemaiah said to Nehemiah,

> *"Let us meet together in the house of God, within the temple, and let us close the doors of the temple, for they are coming to kill you, and they are coming to kill you at night."*
>
> (Nehemiah 6:10)

Nehemiah was encouraged to withdraw to a place of safety. The subtlety was that Shemaiah appeared to be a friend.

"Your life is in danger Nehemiah! Run into the house of God and find safety!" Fear is a formidable weapon, especially when a friend comes pleading caution: "What will happen to you if you stay on this course?" Jesus knew this experience as He was heading for Jerusalem. A friend of His said, "Not the cross Lord." Jesus retorted, "Get behind me, Satan." Peter longed for Jesus to save His own life and others will introduce fear into our hearts as they make similar pleas: "If you go this way it will cost you your home, your job – everything!" Nevertheless, we have a Saviour who said that the way to find our lives was to lose them, thereby delivering us from fear. When we give in to fear we rob ourselves of the wonder of proving God's faithfulness in the midst of difficulty.

Destructive disloyalty

Now we turn to perhaps the ugliest of all strategies used by the devil.

> *"Also in those days many letters went from the nobles of Judah to Tobiah, and Tobiah's letters came to them. For many in Judah were bound by oath to him ... Moreover, they were speaking about his good deeds in my presence and reported my words to him."*
>
> (Nehemiah 6:17–19)

Disloyalty is a wicked, cruel weapon. Many who apparently supported Nehemiah were actually bound to Tobiah, his enemy. One of the greatest agonies that a servant of God has to endure takes place when one who apparently supports you turns out to be disloyal. All other enemies are external, but disloyalty penetrates and wounds the heart.

Once again our Lord Jesus was tempted in all things that we are and His experience is referred to prophetically in Psalm 55:

> *"His speech was smoother than butter,*
> *But his heart was war;*
> *His words were softer than oil,*
> *Yet they were drawn swords."*
>
> (Psalm 55:21)

> *"For it is not an enemy who reproaches me,*
> *Then I could bear it;*
> *Nor is it one who hates me who has exalted himself against me,*
> *Then I could hide myself from him.*
> *But it is you, a man my equal,*
> *My companion and my familiar friend;*

We who had sweet fellowship together
Walked in the house of God in the throng."

(Psalm 55:12–14)

Jesus knew what it was to be betrayed by a kiss.

God hates disloyalty. He delights in covenant love and wants us to be a loyal people. May I ask you, are you loyal or are your feet in two camps? Do you apparently support one church, but really give your allegiance somewhere else? In Nehemiah's day key people were involved, such as some of the nobles. Tragically, we can find some today who promise their allegiance to their pastor, but who still go to others complaining, "We really do not like the way in which this man is taking our church. I'm going to retain my membership so as to withstand him and hold the church on course."

Alternatively, it might be that you belong to a church that does not want to embrace spiritual renewal and restoration. You remain there even though you have no heart for it or faith that it will ever change. In fact, you enjoy more fellowship with a midweek charismatic group than you do with the church you attend on Sundays. You attend the church, but express no true loyalty to it.

I would like to suggest that we cannot have a foot in each camp. Either way we will hurt our brothers by being double-minded. If churches choose to close their doors to charismatic worship they must also be prepared to recognise the fact that they are also closing their doors to charismatic worshippers who must be free to go and find fellowship where they will. It is hardly fair to then describe them as divisive.

God wants us to be loyal people. He wants us to be wholeheartedly committed to a local church. We must be real and make up our minds, and give consistent loyalty to a church and leadership that we can support fully.

Actually, where there is true Christian grace, this can be accomplished without pain and backlash. Men can honestly and humbly agree to differ and go their separate ways, and thankfully, this has often happened. Tragically, however, there has also often been pain and usually it would be true to say that neither party could claim to be free from sin in the way that things have been handled.

However, even though Nehemiah was confronted by powerful obstacles to his progress, he overcame them all. We have noted that he was initially fortified to cope with the task before him. Now we must turn to see how he withstood Satan in the various disguises that have been mentioned.

So We Built the Wall

How did Nehemiah overcome this barrage of attacks? In his determination to rebuild the walls he brushed aside every assault that Satan hurled at him.

He overcame mockery very simply by just getting on with the job. They laughed at Nehemiah. They said, "They cannot build on all this rubbish. If a fox ran up it, it would fall over." Nehemiah gave the best possible answer: he built the wall. When people mock you, your best response is to "build the wall" and be true to your convictions. You do not need to retaliate or try to vindicate yourself. Simply build up the walls of God in your life.

You Christian ladies with non-Christian husbands, you young people who have been saved at university and have come home to your non-believing parents – do not argue! Just build the walls. Let your life shine. Let people observe that the wall is being built as your character develops. Be respectful, sensitive, righteous and clean. Do not become easily offended.

Inwardly Nehemiah said, "Hear, O Lord! (*You* listen because *I* haven't got time! I'm building the wall!)" He did not get taken up with the mockery; he did not allow himself to be affected by it. Having mourned, he was now fortified. They could mock as much as they liked – he just built the wall.

Finally, the fact that the wall stood was proof that God was with Nehemiah. The same must be true for the current work of restoration in the Church. By all means let us graciously answer when we are asked questions, but let us keep on building, let us stay on course, keep going, keep working, and let the fruit speak for itself.

Then Nehemiah overcame the compromise by replying, *"I am doing a great work and cannot come down. Why should the work stop while I leave it and come down to you?"* (Nehemiah 6:3). There is so much discussion today. So many groups and committees want to have yet another meeting of evangelical leaders to discuss all that is happening. We have to be very selective or else we shall be forever on committees discussing what might happen next!

Nehemiah said, "I am doing a great work. I cannot come down. I cannot be forever debating the implication of what I'm doing. I have to obey God and fulfil His purpose." He was not going to be hoodwinked into merely talking about it.

Perhaps the phrase "I am doing a great work. I cannot come down," reminds you of another man? His opponents said to Him, "If you are some great one why don't you come down?" From the cross He would have answered, "I am doing a great work. I will not come down."

Dear friends, we have to identify with the cross. It can be very flattering to be invited to committees to discuss the implications of our work for the Church today, but we need to allow God to help us to know when to go and when to say, "Sorry, but I'm about a great work. I cannot come down. I cannot be forever discussing whether I should make more work more acceptable to the Church at large."

After this attempt for compromise followed the lies. Amazingly, Nehemiah seemed comparatively untroubled by them. He dismissed them: *"Such things as you are saying have not been done, but you are inventing them in your own mind"* (Nehemiah 6:8). This was the end of it. We must emulate him in this. We cannot be taken up with chasing these mysterious allegations or trying to unravel where they all start. Just as Nehemiah did not seem to become preoccupied with them or thrown off course, neither must we be. We must press on!

Next came fear. Nehemiah's answer was clear: *"Should a man like me flee? And could one such as I go into the temple to save his life? I will not go in!"* (Nehemiah 6:11). What a mighty answer! Arrogant? No, he was not arrogant. He has a sense of destiny. He had no intention of running away or being diverted.

After this followed the fifth line of attack – disloyalty. The story provides no answer to disloyalty, however. Nehemiah's heart was broken. Those of you whose hearts have been broken through the disloyalty of those whom you thought you could trust know the agony. You know what it feels like. There is no answer. You have to learn to bear it and make sure that the seed of bitterness is not sown in your spirit. If someone lets you down beware the root of bitterness that can grow up and spoil not only you, but everyone who comes near you as well. It may hurt, but you must not allow your spirit to be soured.

I notice that Nehemiah learned this lesson very quickly. In the very next chapter (Nehemiah 7:2) we find that when the wall is rebuilt and the doors set in place, the gatekeepers, the singers and the Levites are appointed: *"I put Hanani my brother, and Hananiah the commander of the fortress, in charge of Jerusalem, for he was a faithful man and feared God more than many."*

When we are wounded by the disloyal we must make sure that the next time we build on loyal people. This is what Nehemiah did. He did not react; he simply made sure that the next man he built on was loyal and feared the Lord. Those to whom God will entrust responsibility may not appear to be as significant as the nobles who were disloyal, they may not be public figures, but they must be loyal men of integrity who fear God.

Such a man as I

What made Nehemiah so steadfast? What kept him going through such opposition? Firstly, it was his *call*: "Such a man as I." He was not arrogant or full of self-importance, but he was aware that God had apprehended him. In his time of deep sorrow concerning the situation in Jerusalem, God met with him and fortified him by the Holy Spirit. He knew he had been chosen.

We can be fortified by similar truth. He has chosen us before the world was formed to be holy and blameless before Him. He has predestined us. We become strong when we realise that God, out of His great wisdom and knowledge, has reached down to us through eternal ages. He has chosen us. We may be weak and feeble, but He has chosen to use us. For this reason we can say, "I am not going to flee. Should such a man as I flee? God has chosen me!"

In Philippians 3 the apostle Paul introduces us to the most wonderful "that" in the Bible:

> "*I press on so that I may lay hold of that for which also I was laid hold of by Christ Jesus.*"
>
> (Philippians 3:12)

Paul is saying, "Eternal God laid hold of me. I was a rebel; I was an opponent of the gospel, and Christ took hold of me."

If you are a Christian then this is true of you too. Your conversion may not have been very dramatic; you may not have seen a light blazing around you, but if you are a Christian the verse is still true. Christ laid hold of you. It doesn't matter if you say, "But I came from a Christian home." There are plenty of people who have come from Christian homes and have not followed on to know the Lord. But for every one of us who does know the Lord, the truth is that Christ laid hold of us. There is a "that" tied up with your life and mine – "*that* for which Christ Jesus took hold of me."

Paul said that he was pressing after this. His consuming passion was to lay hold of *that* for which Christ laid hold of him. This was the all-consuming passion of his life. Paul had a destiny and a dignity. He was not just being thrown around by the circumstances of life. And neither are you in this world of cynicism and indifference where people ask despairingly, "Who can really change anything?" People feel so hopeless, even in our democratic system. What can we do? Knowing that God has taken hold of us makes all the difference. He has taken hold of us for a purpose, to give us a destiny. We must reply, "I am going to take hold of that for which you took hold of me." Nehemiah was aware that he was a called person like this.

When Nehemiah responded so zealously he found a whole company of people responding with him. His passion was to rebuild Jerusalem and when he arrived on the scene he discovered a whole army of people who said, "Let us arise and build." They had a corporate sense of destiny. Today, many also have a corporate sense of destiny and God is doing a great work in which we feel involved.

For decades the Church has been in the doldrums, but now God is rebuilding her and we are part of this activity of His Spirit. Thousands are being affected. In His mercy God is using us. How can we be taken up with lesser things? The King of Glory is going to make His Church shine again and He has involved us in His great plan. We are helping to prepare the way.

But we are not anything special. Nehemiah was nothing, but

by virtue of his call and his awareness of this call he said, "Should such a man as I flee? I am in the will of God." May I ask, does the will of God grip and thrill you? Nehemiah could not escape God's call on his life, but embraced it with total commitment and used it as a weapon to overcome every enemy. He was armed with purpose – not aimless and therefore vulnerable.

Total commitment

Secondly, the call was matched by commitment. Nehemiah 4:23 reports: *"Neither I, my brothers, my servants, nor the men of the guard who followed me, none of us took off our clothes, each took his weapon even to the water."* The sword and the trowel! We are going to build the Church in the same way. We are going to raise this house in the midst of our enemies who do not want us to. With sword and trowel we shall fight and build. Some people built during the day and were on guard duty all night. They were totally committed to the work. Why? Because they were convinced that it was a great project. Are you committed to a great project of glorifying Jesus on the earth and saving poor sinners? Or do you think that the Church is simply a nice place to attend? I rejoice to see more and more people taking up the challenge of wholehearted commitment to Christ and His Church.

Remember the Lord

Thirdly, Nehemiah reassured the people: *"Do not be afraid of them; remember the Lord who is great and awesome, and fight . . . "* (Nehemiah 4:14). What a mighty statement this is. We need a revelation of our great and terrible God and then we need to fight, assured of His sufficiency. Be strong in the Lord and in the power of His might. If you are not strong in the Lord the devil will penetrate with his fiery darts. Be strong because you *must*

be and be strong because you *can* be! Remember the Lord, who
is great and terrible, and fight. The God of heaven will give us
success if we have absolute confidence in Him.

Comradeship

Fourthly, Nehemiah grouped men together. In panic some
were terrified of being overrun: *"They will come up against us
from every place where you may turn"* (Nehemiah 4:12). So
Nehemiah *"stationed men in the lowest parts of the space behind
the wall, the exposed places, and I stationed the people in families
with their swords, spears and bows"* (Nehemiah 4:13). What
comradeship as they all stood together! Sometimes they were
separated from one another because of the length of the wall, so
Nehemiah instructed them to sound the trumpet in the event of
an attack: *"At whatever place you hear the sound of the trumpet,
rally to us there"* (Nehemiah 4:20).

This comradeship should characterise our church life. We
should not go through pressures alone. Of course, our personal
relationship with the Lord is vital to our spiritual life, but we
also need to blow the trumpet so that people can rush to help
and take the load.

I remember when my wife was about five months pregnant
with one of our children and I was at a conference. Suddenly
the membrane containing the fluid around the baby was
punctured. My wife immediately took to her bed and tele-
phoned some ladies from the church that promptly rushed in,
took our children and looked after everything. The doctor later
said the child might easily have been lost had it not been for my
wife lying down so quickly. Because of the help of our dear
friends our baby survived! My wife blew the trumpet and the
people rushed to help. Is your church like this? Or does nobody
even know that you belong? God wants His Church to be a

community where, if you pick up the phone, there are people ready to lend a hand. They rush in and they care! The Church may be growing larger and larger, but there also has to be a company who know you and care for you.

If we are in distress we also need to be increasingly open, not self-sufficient and independent, but willing to ask for help. Don't sweat things out on your own – too proud to be honest – so that when you are asked, "How are things?" you conceal your real need under a superficial "Fine, thank you." God wants us to be more honest than this. When you are under pressure blow the trumpet and cry out for help!

I remember a men's meeting many years ago when a policeman friend of mine arrived utterly exhausted. He turned up a bit late in a crowded room of men and said, "I am shattered." I must confess that at the time I thought, "What a great way to start a meeting!" but as he began to share what he had been through that day the presence of God began to be manifested in the room. There was a beautiful sharing of the load and I still remember that evening as one of our most remarkable times of spiritual breakthrough. Here was a brother blowing his trumpet. He did not conceal his need and instead shared his pain. God owned the reality and we were able to worship Him in Spirit and truth.

Sometimes pressure comes to your part of the wall. If you do not shout we will not necessarily know about it. We must build a sense of comradeship into our relationships.

"Hear me, O God"

Nehemiah's final weapon is clearly seen as that of constant prayer. When you read through the book of Nehemiah you cannot fail to see the many verses where Nehemiah cries, "Hear me, O God!" From the outset he was a man of prayer.

Chapter 1 records his long intercessory prayer and then in chapter 2 we eavesdrop on his meeting with the king: *"What would you request?"* the king asks. A beautiful autobiographical detail follows: *"I prayed to the God of heaven. I said to the king . . . "* (Nehemiah 2:4–5). This is how Nehemiah lived all the time.

Later, Nehemiah had no time to even change his clothes from one day to the next, but he was constantly crying out, "God, hear what my enemy is saying!" Without ceasing he prayed, "Hear me, O God!"

He was constantly asking God to strengthen his hands. Just like Jesus, his prayers were ceaseless. We will never see what God has for us without developing a similar lifestyle of constant prayer to God. This was how Nehemiah overcame and it was how Jesus prevailed. The early disciples learned this lesson from Jesus and devoted themselves to prayer. Prayer underpinned all their activity. It was never dull or routine, but always in the context of gospel advance. On the day of Pentecost they prayed and fire fell! A few days later they prayed and the house shook, and they were freshly filled with the Holy Spirit and boldness. News of Peter's imprisonment inspired them not to storm the jail, but to storm the heavens in earnest intercession, which led to his release. We must similarly bathe all of our activities in believing prayer if we are to enjoy the kind of success that Nehemiah experienced.

So Nehemiah brushed aside every attack that was launched against him. With unwavering determination he pressed towards his goal. He knew God had apprehended him and like Jesus, his food was to do the will of Him who sent him and to finish His work (see John 4:34). Nothing could deflect him from his course. May God inspire in us a similar devotion and determination so that in our day the Church may be restored to beauty and strength, and be a Bride worthy of her wonderful Lord.

CHAPTER 20

Becoming a Community

Having won the battle, what comes next? Nehemiah also needed to form the people into a loving community. When the external battle fades from view we often begin to find problems within. When we are no longer cast against a common enemy we begin to have difficulties with one another. When the enemy is outside we all carry our swords and work together as an army on the frontline, but when the enemy is no longer attacking we notice details that have previously been overlooked – "You didn't lay that brick very well! You just dropped your trowel on my foot!"

We must begin with a fervent determination to be one people. Nehemiah 8:1 tells us that, *"all the people gathered as one man."* This appears again in verse 12 – *"All the people went away to eat, to drink."* It does not say that some of them said, "No, the situation is too serious. We must stay here." The command came: *"Do not be grieved, for the joy of the LORD is your strength"* (Nehemiah 8:10). So they *all* went. They had come down to listen to Ezra and now they all departed to do as they had been told. When they discovered in the law that they should celebrate the Feast of the Tabernacles "the entire assembly did it". Scripture does not say, "Some zealous ones obeyed, but others thought that it wasn't a good idea." No, the entire assembly complied. A mighty unity of purpose took hold of them. We must be motivated like this if we are to see the Church restored.

A "nobody" or a "somebody"?

What are some of the enemies of unity? In 1 Corinthians 12 Paul unexpectedly points out that the first to break the unity are those who disqualify themselves. He tells us that the foot cannot say, *"Because I am not a hand, I am not a part of the body"* (1 Corinthians 12:15). Some of us say, "I am only a foot. No one notices me." What we mean is, "I am no problem to unity really since I am just a nobody." Actually, we bring disunity when we adopt this attitude because a "dead" member is disunited from the living body, thereby frustrating the grace of God in the whole. So Paul says, "Beware of saying you are a nobody."

When we embrace this attitude we begin to take a back seat. Gradually we drift into becoming mere spectators. Uninvolved in the battle, we sit on the terraces and can often find we are being tempted to criticise since we can easily observe other people's errors. Paul's counsel is that we should be united by finding our place in the body and therefore be thoroughly fulfilled!

In the same chapter Paul swings to address the self-important who also bring disunity. Some people are so full of themselves that they do not need others. In conversation they simply wait for you to finish so that they can have their say. Whenever you share your news with them they have information to trump yours! Those who argue, "I have no need of you" display the self-importance that frustrates unity in the Body.

Loving encounters

The fearful who will not confront also bring disunity. When someone is continually offending we must ask God for courage to act. When we do not confront we leave a vulnerable area for the devil, who tempts us to indulge in criticism and gossip. When a third party is critical of the one that you feel is in error you are easily drawn in. So one of the ways we overcome disunity is to find the love and courage to confront others. The Bible says, "Admonish one another" and "Exhort one another every day." If we are going to become a true community or family we have to find grace to speak into one another's lives and overcome the fear of being rejected. Elders in a local church must certainly be able to check one another. If leaders paper over their differences the flock will soon become aware of the cracks.

Free forgiveness

Those who refuse to forgive also prevent true unity. This is so obvious that I do not need to spend a lot of time on it, except to say this: Christians may have many, many faults, but they should excel at forgiving! We should all be magnificent forgivers, even if we fail in other areas. We may not be able to sing or serve, or organise very well, but we should be brilliant at forgiving because we have all been forgiven. If we are not first-class at forgiving then it is questionable whether we really know the grace of God. We should be gold medallists at it!

Another person who breaks unity is the legalist – the one who lives by rules and condemns those who do not. He fragments the body; he lives by a very rigid rulebook and, having been diligent to do that himself, is greatly offended by the freedom of others. Romans 14 warns against such a stance.

We are not to pass judgement on other people's liberty, nor are we to despise other people's consciences. We must allow each man to stand before his God and answer for himself.

A further cause of disunity in a local church is the "watch-dog" who is there ensuring that the pastor "does not take things too far". He feels that he is there to safeguard from error and excess! Such a man brings disunity; he feels that he is serving God, but he is in fact spoiling the progress of that local church.

In longing for unity we must be willing to lose our identity – God treasures the uniqueness of the individual, but He deplores our independence. Are you the one who always demands that everything must be explained to you? Do you insist that you must always be satisfied when leaders invite you to join them in a certain course? Are you responsive or do you reply, "I will do so if God tells me to"? Some are continually defensive, aloof and unwilling just to cast their lot in with God's people. If you are such a person you are frustrating the unity that God seeks. By all means discuss your difficulties, but do not be defensive. Be willing to lose your life in order that you might find it.

Value people for themselves

Sometimes our very zeal for God can condemn others who begin to feel that they are only valued as people in terms of what they can accomplish; they do not feel beloved and precious. God wants us genuinely to rejoice in one another. If we continually pressurise one another to be doing more, the whole Church becomes riddled with striving and self-effort. God wants a unity based on grace that is all embracing, loving and accepting, without a whiff of condemnation.

Will you be determined to be of one heart? It is the priority of the New Testament. Peter says, *"**Above all**, keep fervent in your* *love for one another . . . "* (1 Peter 4:8, emphasis added). Do not just put up with one another, but be fervent in love.

Some argue that the trouble with this sort of church is that the members all think the same, but this is exactly what Paul expected! He exhorts us to be *"made complete in the same mind and in the same judgement"* (1 Corinthians 1:10). Clearly Paul does not mean that we have to become so submissive that we are not allowed to think for ourselves. We can arrive at wholehearted agreement with joy and faith. The New Testament norm is that we are perfectly joined together in one mind and one judgement. For the sake of unity we refuse to indulge in the luxury of being offended, disapproving, critical and intolerant.

For Nehemiah, *"all the people gathered as one man"* (Nehemiah 8:1). To maintain this unity will require all our energies, but this is what the Lord expects of us. Paul pleaded with the Ephesians to be *"diligent to preserve the unity of the Spirit in the bond of peace"* (Ephesians 4:3). In this great chapter are included some of the most glorious descriptions of the Church in the whole Bible. He saw the Body of Christ being built up until we all reach unity in the faith and in the knowledge of the Son of God, and becoming mature, attaining to the whole measure of the fullness of Christ (Ephesians 4:12–13).

However, in order to reach this magnificent conclusion we must *"be completely humble and gentle; be patient, bearing with one another in love"* (Ephesians 4:2 NIV). We must speak the truth in love and, finally, build ourselves up in love as each part does its work (see Ephesians 4:15–16).

All of this requires sustained determination to receive one another as Christ received us and to retain humble attitudes of love and acceptance at all times. Only then will the house of God be restored in glory on the earth and will Jesus receive the praise of which He is worthy.

Building on Truth

The next key factor in forming these returned exiles into a community was supplied by Ezra the teacher who *"brought the law before the assembly of men, women and all who could listen with understanding"* (Nehemiah 8:2). It was crucial that their recovery programme and expression of loving unity was based on the revealed Word of God. Ezra was a vital restoration figure!

In seeking a recovery of the New Testament Church life we are not just arguing for the reinstatement of speaking in tongues and prophesying. We want to see the Bible restored to its rightful place as the final authority for church life. Ezra was not dismissed as "just a Bible teacher". On the contrary, they built him a podium in the centre of the square and *"all the people gathered as one man"* to hear him. His teaching brought a genuine touch of revival, which they had not previously known.

Some people in the early days of the charismatic movement were so hostile to the perils of the one-man ministry that they turned against prepared teaching in favour of a spontaneous form of "body ministry". They tried to live on a diet of spontaneous sharing and regarded prepared Bible exposition as outdated. This was, of course, a tragic mistake.

I recall attending a church where, after a lively time of praise, one brother stood and exhorted everybody to be real. He then gave a five-minute talk on openness and transparency. After more praise, a second brother rose to his feet and to my amazement called us to be *really* real! No other preaching took place. The Church cannot expect to grow on a diet of exhortations to be "really real".

Some expressed their frustration with their former experience of cold Bible teaching by arguing that the early Christians had no Bible. It was argued that throughout the first centuries of the Church Christians did not carry a big black Bible with them, therefore we also should simply "be yourself in the Spirit"! Some charismatics have clearly given the impression that they are anti-Bible.

If, however, we see the book of Nehemiah as a guidebook to restoration, we could never take this path as we see the central role that Ezra fulfilled.

We must always remember that Jesus came as a teacher sent from God. He went everywhere teaching the kingdom. Even after He had been raised from the dead He continued to teach. If ever there was a time when teaching would seem unnecessary it was then, but He didn't just turn up and say, "Look, I'm back!" Instead, He opened the Scriptures and, "starting with Moses and all the prophets, He spoke to them of all the things concerning Himself." It was not enough to just appear. The apostles were not persecuted by their opponents for filling Jerusalem with their miracles, but for filling Jerusalem with their *teaching*.

Although it could be argued that first-century Christians had no Bibles, it is clearly recorded that they devoted themselves to the apostles' doctrine and that Paul claimed to have taught them day and night, clearly instructing Timothy to guard the form of sound doctrine and to pass it on to others who were able, in turn, to communicate it faithfully. On one occasion we read of the apostle Paul preaching all night, interrupted only by a swift resurrection job on a boy who fell from the window! Paul would hardly have been content to give the impression that all the young Christians needed to do was "to live from their spirit".

Truth to safeguard us

The Word of God must take central place to safeguard us from errors, both old and new. We are warned that in the last days there will be doctrines of demons; there will be some strange new ideas that people with itching ears will follow. Many are already around today. We need to be clearly grounded in the Scriptures so that we are not vulnerable to counterfeit signs and wonders.

Likewise, we must beware of old strange doctrines that explain away the Bible and give greater place to tradition than they do to the revealed truth. Jesus said to the men of His day, "You have a fine way of disregarding the Word of God so that you might keep your own traditions" (see Matthew 15:6). We need to bring every tradition in our church life to this book and ask, "Is it in the book? If it is not in the Bible, why do we do it?"

The Word of God will inspire a true knowledge of God and to know Him is eternal life. We need to know objective truth. We rejoice in the intuitive knowledge that comes from the Spirit and reveals Christ to us, but the Bible tells us wonderful things about God which we would not know intuitively. We would not know what the cross means if the Bible didn't explain it to us. Other events in Jesus' life and throughout the Bible are only understood as we seek God's own interpretation of these events as recorded in Scripture.

If we bow to the authority of Scripture instead of bowing to almighty tradition we would see what church worship is meant to be like. We would see the place of apostles and prophets if we would only ask, "What does the book say?"

Does it suggest that the ministries listed in Ephesians 4 should cease by the end of the first century? Does the Bible actually say that there were only twelve apostles? It does not! We must bow to the authority of Scripture in our restoration recovery and reformation. The Reformation of Luther's day provided a glorious dawn, yet still left many shadows in Church life. For a full recovery of New Testament Church life we must yield ourselves to the Word of God as they did in Ezra's day.

The truth sets us free

Knowing the truth releases us. We need to know what happened to us when Jesus died. Gospel truth not only prepares us for heaven – it releases us for life in the present. We need to know that our old self was crucified with Him and that He who had died is free from sin (see Romans 6:6–7). Many are condemned because they do not know. Many are still living under the oppression of the law because they do not know that Christ is the end of the law to everyone who believes. Many live under a heavy cloud because they do not know that there is no condemnation for those who are in Christ Jesus.

Through the very great and precious promises God has given us everything we need for life and godliness (see 2 Peter 1:3–4). The victory that overcomes the world is our faith and faith comes through hearing the Word of God. The Word of God, then, is central to restoration, both in our individual lives and in our church life.

I remember being in a cathedral in Barcelona some years ago. I had gone to visit my sister who was a missionary there and I had a little time before catching the plane home. I was sitting in the cathedral looking around when in came a frail old lady dressed in black, her back bent double. She bought a candle, lit it and placed it in front of a statue. Putting a veil over her head, she sat there looking up at the statue – and I thought of the words of Jesus. There must have been many things that that lady needed. She was poor, she was bent over, but the thing that she needed more than anything else was this: that someone would teach her many things.

> *"When Jesus went ashore, He saw a large crowd, and He felt compassion for them because they were like sheep without a shepherd; and He began to teach them many things."*
>
> (Mark 6:34)

CHAPTER 22

What a Celebration!

Next to be restored was the celebration of the Feast of Tabernacles, or the Feats of Booths. They went into the hill country and cut down branches from the trees to make booths, or tents, and for a whole week they lived in them. But why? They were remembering their true identity. They were saying, "Although we are building this city we are actually a pilgrim people." Though they were remembering something solid and substantial, they had to remember as true children of God that earthly Jerusalem was not their final destination. Abraham, their pilgrim father, with the eye of faith had seen a city with foundations whose maker and builder was God. From that day on Abraham no longer lived in Ur of the Chaldees, but made his home in a tent. Every time they celebrated the Feast of Tabernacles they were remembering the same truth.

The same must be true for us. Although we want to build something substantial in our generation, our eyes must still be focused on the glorious hope that will be revealed to us at the coming of our Lord Jesus. We have the blessed hope of a magnificent future! We must constantly remember that we are a people whose roots are somewhere else and that we are only here temporarily. The very essence of a tent is impermanence; put up in an hour, blown down in five minutes!

Paul tells us, *"*[Christ] *gave himself for our sins so that He might rescue us from this present evil age . . . "* (Galatians 1:4). We are not only delivered from sin, guilt and punishment, but delivered out of this present age. Again we are told, "Let those of us who have dealings with this world be as though we had no dealings with it." We must not let the world squeeze us into its mould. The night is almost gone and day is at hand! We are children of the day, not of the night, so do not get taken up with something that is going to vanish in a moment of time. The book of Revelation tells us that great Babylon, that mighty city, will crumble to dust in one hour. We live in a passing age – don't get caught up in it!

The international, worldwide outpouring of the Holy Spirit is heralding and preparing the way for the return of Christ; it is almost here. Why give our lives to lesser things? Let us remember where our hope lies. Paul said, *"we exult in hope of the glory of God"* (Romans 5:2). Our ultimate hope must not be focused only on the restoration of the Church, but on the coming of Jesus. We may prophesy, but we only prophesy in part. There may be tongues, but they will cease. When the perfect comes the partial disappears. Now we see in a mirror dimly, but then face to face.

Some time ago I listened to a tape by A.W. Tozer. I had never heard this twentieth-century prophet on tape before. His writings are challenging enough! His address was on Isaiah 6 and I wondered if I was ready to hear it. Apprehensively, I switched it on. He began, "Tonight I am going to speak about the holiness of God. I am a fool. No one should speak about it for we know nothing about it." This spiritual giant of a man declared himself a fool to speak of that which he knew nothing about! Dear friends, we know a little pinprick of truth and it has transformed us. What will it be like when we see Him? In moments of worship we catch glimpses of His glory, but what will it be to see Him face to face?

God may have given you a lovely home or a healthy body but remember, it is really only a tent:

> *"For we know that if the earthly tent which is our house is torn down, we have a building from God, a house not made with hands, eternal in the heavens."*
>
> (2 Corinthians 5:1)

God may have blessed us with material provision, but let us make sure that our eyes are fixed on the unseen and the eternal.

As the Israelites dwelt in tents for their Feast of Tabernacles they were remembering their true identity as the people of God. We too shall be seen as different to society around about us, not simply by building successful churches, but by having a totally different approach to life because we have no fear of death and are looking forward to meeting Jesus.

Rediscover your roots

In the ninth chapter of Nehemiah we read that the next thing the Israelites did was to recount their history. We need to know our roots. Sometimes, hearing charismatics pray, you would think that the Church only started in our generation! Many of us have no grasp of what God has been doing through the ages. Our prayer and praise times often reflect this short-sighted view. It is pointless for us to live in the past, but let us be clear: the Church has not just arrived on the scene! We have a wonderful heritage! If we want to know our identity we must rediscover our roots and be aware of church history.

When I was first saved I lived on a diet of biographies! I thank God for men like Hudson Taylor, Murray McCheyne, George Müller, Praying Hyde, George Whitefield, to name a few. We have a wonderful family tree! Do you know about them? Let me encourage you to read the lives of such men and rub shoulders with these giants. They are our forefathers and we need to rediscover the histories of these amazing men and women. You will feel very much at home with many of them. Read Ian Murray and rediscover the "Puritan hope". Their hope coincides very much with yours. Read *The Pilgrim Church* by Broadbent and you will find that you are part of a great ongoing move of God. Study it. Be stimulated and strengthened by it.

As the pioneering settlers were restored in Jerusalem they must have derived great comfort as they rehearsed their history together, as recorded in Nehemiah 9. They were able to catch the grand sweep of God's purposes and see something of the overall plan of God, thereby underlining their own sense of identity.

Triumphant worship

With a growing sense of purpose they completed the building of the walls and arranged a celebratory dedication – a festival of praise! They brought the Levites to Jerusalem so that they might celebrate the dedication with hymns of thanksgiving and the music of cymbals, harps and lyres. Nehemiah arranged for the leaders of Judah to mount the wall and appointed two great choirs to march around it.

Tobiah said that even if a fox had climbed up these walls they would have fallen down and yet here were choirs marching on them. What a day of celebration!

When they concluded their triumphant march they offered great sacrifices and rejoiced. Even the women and children rejoiced so that the joy of Jerusalem was heard from afar. How fitting it was that they should celebrate in this way. And how much more fitting it is for the Church of God to display joy that is unspeakable and full of glory. Triumphant praise will be one of the marks of the Church in the last days. It should have been so throughout the ages!

When Paul was looking for this distinctive sign of a true church, which would mark it out from others he said, *"For we are the true circumcision, who worship in the Spirit of God . . . "* (Philippians 3:3). He could have used so many different phrases to describe the true Church. He could have said, "For it is we who are the circumcision, we who believe in the atonement" and this would have been very true. He could have argued, "It is we who are the circumcision who have direct access to the early apostles." But instead he said, *"We are the true circumcision, who worship in the Spirit of God and glory in Christ Jesus and put no confidence in the flesh."*

So if you arrive in a town wondering where the true church of God is, a biblical way of identifying them, according to Paul's letter, is that the true people of God will be those who are worshipping in the Spirit. This will mark them out – it will be one of the identifiable things about them. Paul could have said that the true circumcision were those in true doctrine, but actually, if you find a company who are *truly* worshipping in the Spirit, you have found a church that has already spent time in sorting out many other things. And if they are worshipping in Spirit and truth, love and unity must be prevailing.

Worshipping by the Spirit does not come easily to a local church. It does not happen overnight. The book of Nehemiah does not start with marching, rejoicing choirs and orchestras on top of the walls, although it does get there eventually!

I rejoice to see the growing worship groups in local churches today. It is very thrilling to see the diversity of instruments and to see young people contributing to worship.

I well remember the first Sunday when loud clashing cymbals were played at my home church in Brighton. As we sang one of the great hymns I suddenly saw a light flash and wondered what it was. It wasn't a heavenly visitation, but light being reflected on two large cymbals as they were being taken out of a bag! We were singing one of those magnificent old hymns like "Praise the Lord, His glories show" and the "hallelujah" that concludes each line was accompanied by a crash of those shining cymbals. It was wonderful! There are some instruments that speak of the majesty of God and, whilst the old harmonium isn't one of them, the clashing cymbal most certainly is! God is worthy of all our enthusiasm and the combination of all our skills.

A revolution has been taking place! Englishmen, reserved and respectable, who formerly kept their hands battened resolutely down to their sides, have become hand-clapping, hand-raising enthusiasts!

Joyful praise and heartfelt worship have replaced the formal hymn singing, which used to be just a prelude to the preaching in most churches. "Participation" has become a key word that supersedes passivity. Growing numbers of people are taking part in congregational worship with spoken and sung prophecies, tongues and interpretation, shared visions, or in playing musical instruments among growing church music groups.

The manifestation of the presence of God has become almost breathtaking in its intensity, evoking shouts of joys and tears of devoted adoration.

Prophetic songs have multiplied, focusing our vision on the city of God, the government of Christ and the purpose of God to reach the nations through a glorious Church. Beautiful worship songs have melted our hearts and helped us to recognise the Lord's personal and intimate love for us. We have stood or knelt in His presence with great delight. Hymn boards and bored hymn singers have largely become relics of the past!

It has become so edifying to sing passages of Scripture set to music so that we are meditating on the truth as well as worshipping the Lord. The Lord is seeking those who will worship Him in Spirit and truth, and I believe He is finding them in increasing numbers.

Praise and worship have become not only an expression of love but also a declaration of war as we freshly commit ourselves to our King and His kingdom and, as His Bride, make ourselves ready for His return with heartfelt joy.

God is gradually filling out our worship. It is becoming more worthy of Him. Restored worship is one of the most significant features that characterise our church life:

> *"The joy of Jerusalem was heard from afar."*
>
>   (Nehemiah 12:43)

CHAPTER 23

Throw Him Out!

I was greatly tempted to forget that after the triumphant choirs of Nehemiah 12 come the disappointments of Nehemiah 13. How lovely it would be to conclude at the end of chapter 12 while the choirs were still singing! Chapter 13 seems such an embarrassing anti-climax. As I prayed, "Please Father, may I finish on chapter 12?" I felt God say to me quite clearly, "No, you may not. Not only may you not finish on that note of glory and praise, but you must look at chapter 13 and faithfully teach it." In the final analysis life simply doesn't consist of Feasts of Tabernacles.

God instigated three festivals in the Jewish national year when they would gather to Him without distraction. But God knows, and we know, that the real crunch comes not when we are singing praise with thousands of others, but when we return to our normal, real-life situations. Nehemiah 13 uncompromisingly reminds us of this truth.

It recounts how Nehemiah returned to Babylon. Then, after a period of time (how long is not absolutely clear) he came back to Jerusalem and discovered that, to his horror, the people of God had backslidden from the euphoria of those earlier days. They had failed to retain their pioneering clarity.

A little leaven

In Nehemiah's absence *"Eliashib the priest ... being related to Tobiah, had prepared a large room for him where formerly they put ... the utensils, and the tithes of grain, wine and oil prescribed for the Levites"* (Nehemiah 13:4–5).

On his return, however, Nehemiah recorded:

> *"I came to Jerusalem and learned about the evil that Eliashib had done for Tobiah, by preparing a room for him in the courts of the house of God. It was very displeasing to me, so I threw all of Tobiah's household goods out of the room. Then I gave an order and they cleansed the rooms; and I returned there the utensils of the house of God with the grain offerings and the frankincense."*
> (Nehemiah 13:7–9)

Nehemiah had retuned to find Tobiah housed in a room within the very house of God. Tobiah had sent letters to frighten Nehemiah and some had been disloyally bound by oath to him. He had been a constant thorn in Nehemiah's side and now here he was right back in the centre of the life of Zion in the house of God!

What is the New Testament significance for us in this picture? As I was before God I felt that He reminded me of a clear parallel – an enemy of the gospel, first of all mocking, then opposing and finally, trying to join in the very life of the church. It seems to me that the apostle Paul had to fight his own "Tobiah" who appeared as *legalism*.

Let me explain what I mean. At first, the legalists, personified by the Pharisees, heard and withstood John the Baptist as he prepared the way for the Lord. Like Tobiah, they claimed to be the true people of the land. They were Abraham's sons! When Jesus arrived on the scene they withstood Him. They mocked

Him as the son of a carpenter; they noticed that no serious Pharisee was following Him. Later, as Jesus' following was gathering momentum their mockery changed to serious debate. They tried to catch Him in His words; they brought clever arguments asking, "Should we pay taxes to Caesar or not?" They tried to force Him into debate. They told lies and brought many false accusations.

Later, as the early Church triumphed with multitudes being converted, many priests became obedient to the faith. Later still, thousands of Jews believed, many of whom were zealous for the law (see Acts 21:20). Gradually, many of these converted priests brought their legalism right into the young Church in Jerusalem. Legalism spelled troubled for Paul and he fought a running battle with this loathsome blight, which had found its way where it did not belong.

Paul's letter to the Galatians handles the matter very fully. Paul had planted a pure church in Galatia through his gospel preaching. Later, he was stunned to learn that legalism was creeping in so he wrote to them, *"Did you suffer so many things in vain?"* (Galatians 3:4). You could ask the same of those with Nehemiah: "You worked so hard to restore the city. Have you suffered so much for nothing? You have invited Tobiah right back in!" Paul was horrified that the Galatians had freshly embraced the law.

> *"At that time, when you did not know God, you were slaves to those which by nature are no gods. But now that you have come to know God, or rather to be known by God, how is it that you turn back again to the weak and worthless elemental things, to which you desire to be enslaved all over again? You observe days and months and seasons and years. I fear for you, that perhaps I have laboured over you in vain."*

(Galatians 4:8–11)

The gospel had brought them into freedom. Was it all in vain? Had they subjected themselves to the same enslaving once again? A few lines later Paul asked:

> *"Tell me, you who want to be under law, do you not listen to the law? For it is written that Abraham had two sons, one by the bondwoman and one by the free woman. But the son by the bondwoman was born according to the flesh, and the son by the free woman through the promise. This is allegorically speaking, for these women are two covenants: one proceeding from Mount Sinai bearing children who are to be slaves; she is Hagar. Now this Hagar is Mount Sinai in Arabia and corresponds to the present Jerusalem, for she is in slavery with her children. But the Jerusalem above is free; she is our mother . . .*
>
> *And you brethren, like Isaac, are children of promise. But as at that time he who was born according to the flesh persecuted him who was born according to the Spirit, so it is now also. But what does the Scripture say? 'Cast out the bondwoman and her son, for the son of the bondwoman shall not be an heir with the son of the free woman.' So then, brethren, we are not children of a bondwoman, but of the free woman. It was for freedom that Christ set us free; therefore keep standing firm and do not be subject again to a yoke of slavery."*
>
> (Galatians 4:21–26, 28–5:1)

How similar to the situation faced by Nehemiah! A church that was pure, the product of the gospel, had once again embraced legalism – that product of human endeavour with all its rules and regulations, observing certain rules, wearing certain clothes, endeavouring to obey certain laws. Nehemiah's answer to Tobiah was to say, "Throw him out and all his furniture with him!" Paul's answer to the law was, "Cast out the bond woman and her son."

We are born again that we might reign in life, not through laws that we impose on ourselves, for the law will always condemn us (as Romans 7 makes perfectly clear). If we seek sanctification through observance of the law we will ultimately meet with frustration and condemnation. The law cannot sanctify us. God gave the law to lead us to Christ.

> *"Christ is the end of the law for righteousness to everyone who believes."*
>
> (Romans 10:4)

And *"we have been released from the Law"* (Romans 7:6). Although the law will never pass away Christians can rejoice that they have died to the law through the body of Christ!

A new husband

There is no way into joy, freedom and peace of mind by being married to the law. The law is totally impotent. As Paul argues in Galatians 3,

> *". . . if a law had been given which was able to impart life, then righteousness would indeed have been based on law."*
>
> (Galatians 3:21)

The law cannot impart life. The law can point out our faults and show us where we are going wrong, but it does not give life. It only leads to condemnation.

When we are saved Jesus invites us to come to Him. He unites us with Him in His death to the law. We are also united to Him in resurrection life and have now become His Bride. Whereas our old husband, the law, merely told us what to do, but never gave us life or help, Jesus says, "Abide in Me, and I in you, and you will bear much fruit" (see Matthew 15:4). Jesus is a life-imparting husband! He can plant His seed in me and bring forth fruit. So, I grow up in Christ not by returning to law, but by developing my relationship with Jesus.

Nehemiah was outraged – "How did Tobiah get back into the temple?" Paul was outraged – "Cast out the bond woman and her child!" We must learn to cast out legalism and have nothing to do with it. Instead, we must learn to live in close fellowship with the Lord Jesus and have His living words in us. His words are Spirit and life. Feed on them. He is the Bread of Life. He is food for your soul. His word brings forth faith. Get to know Jesus, love Him and obey Him. Do these things and you will be fruitful. For the letter kills but the Spirit gives life!

CHAPTER 24

Till the Day Dawns

Another disappointment for Nehemiah on his return to Jerusalem was that the people had not continued to tithe faithfully in support of Levites:

> *"The portions of the Levites had not been given them, so that the Levites and the singers who performed the service had gone away, each to his own field."*

(Nehemiah 13:10)

They had begun to lose their corporate vision and had stopped giving.

Originally, as pioneers, they had left their homes in Babylon and risked everything. Returning to Jerusalem had cost them dearly. Nevertheless, they had begun well in their commitment to tithing to the Levites. Gradually they began to settle. Now the walls were up they were secure and the people's commitment had run dry so that the Levites had to resort to working on their fields.

God had not planned for them to have any land originally. The eleven tribes had territory of their own and gave a tenth of their income to keep the Levites, but now this God-ordained means of support had evaporated.

Our financial giving often reflects our wholeheartedness. It authenticates our devotion to Christ and to His Church. Where our treasure is, there our heart is also. It has been said that Christianity is the most secular religion in the world. In other words, the Bible says more about hard cash than any other religious book. Other religious books trade in philosophies and abstract thoughts, whereas the Bible speaks to real people in the real twenty-first century, making it plain that if we cannot honour God with our giving there is something wrong with our faith, love and sense of commitment.

We must not only be generous givers, but also committed, regular givers to our local church. Our chief responsibility is giving to our home base. If we have made sure we have fulfilled our responsibilities there, we are also free to give further afield. But, if we have godly leadership, why not trust them to channel resources around the world. Your part is to show your faithfulness to your local work by systematically giving there.

It has to be asked whether ministers are receiving a proper wage. Through the system of tithing the Levites received just above the average of the income of the other tribes. It could be argued, therefore, that a minister should earn something consistent with the average salary in his congregation, with a little more for the extra expenses he incurs. Some churches argue that they only give a small salary, but that they do provide a house. In other words, the man has a tied house with all the insecurity that this brings and which he loses at retirement and can never call his own. We need to look into this. It is very difficult for ministers to preach about giving because of the obvious implications and they can be accused of feathering their own nests. It is a simple matter for them to preach about justification by faith, evangelism or holiness, but it is not easy for them to take on the theme of giving. Perhaps you are one of those who have the responsibility of deciding your minister's salary. Let me encourage you to look realistically and, if necessary, radically at the whole subject, and care properly for the man whom God has put among you to serve you in the Word. As Paul said to the Corinthians, *"Just as you excel in everything . . . excel in this grace of giving"* (2 Corinthians 8:7 NIV).

Being different

The third area that Nehemiah encountered on his return was the people's departure from keeping the Sabbath. The people were treading out the wine presses, bringing in sacks of grain and loading them onto donkeys – and all this on the Sabbath day. Sabbath observance was one of those features that made the Israelites distinctive from all the other nations. Other nations worked and bought and sold on the Sabbath, but Israel was to be different in this particular way. They were not to be involved in any of these routine activities from Friday evening, when they began to celebrate the Sabbath, right through to Saturday night.

Merchants and traders from other nations expected "business as usual" seven days a week and in Nehemiah's absences the Jews had gradually conceded to their style. The Sabbath day in Jerusalem had become like any other day.

Nehemiah immediately rebuked them and ordered the doors to be shut. When some tradesmen actually camped outside the city he threatened to lay hands on them and placed guards on the gates.

We must, of course, understand that the Sabbath was something that was instituted for the Jewish nation. Colossians 2:16–17 says,

> *"Therefore no one is to act as your judge in regard to food or drink or in respect to a festival or a new moon or a Sabbath*

day – things which are a mere shadow of what is to come; but
the substance belongs to Christ."

Or, as Paul argues elsewhere,

"One person regards one day above another, another regards
every day alike. Each person must be fully convinced in his
own mind."

(Romans 14:5)

Paul's conclusion is that each one should be fully convinced in
his own mind. It is evident, then, that the New Testament does
not regard keeping the Sabbath as a vital theme in the way that
it obviously was in the Old Testament.

The enduring fact is that the people of God are meant to be
different! We are to be *"blameless and innocent, children of God*
above reproach in the midst of a crooked and perverse generation,
among whom you appear as lights in the world" (Philippians 2:15).
We are to *"keep [our] behaviour excellent among the Gentiles . . . "*
(1 Peter 2:12). Peter goes on to argue, *"For the time already past is*
sufficient for you to have carried out the desire of the Gentiles . . . they
are surprised that you do not run with them . . . " (1 Peter 4:3–4).
Are they surprised? Do you cause surprises at work and at
home? Peter says that this is one of the marks of the Christian –
he causes his colleagues to be surprised! You used to be heavily
involved, but now you have changed. That past time was
sufficient. God expects the Christian to live a completely
different lifestyle.

Grace to say "no"

We must not consider the grace of God to mean "easy
believing". God's grace is not meant to be blurring the edge

of our commitment to holy living. In fact, Paul reminds us in Titus 2 that *"the grace of God ... has appeared ... It teaches us to say 'No' to ungodliness ... to live self-controlled, upright and godly lives in this present age"* (Titus 2:11–12 NIV). The rest of the world may be bent on destruction, but the grace of God teaches us to say "no". We are called upstream against the flow. In our generation young people will often be called to demonstrate the grace of God by saying "no".

These Jews had originally been so zealous to build the walls and so keen to march around them celebrating the distinctiveness that they represented, yet all that labour to build the walls had become futile because they now allowed unrighteousness to come through the gates. Like Joseph, we are to be resolute in refusing evil.

In Nehemiah's absence the returned exiles had become so careless about retaining their distinctiveness that their children no longer knew how to speak the language of Judah and were beginning to speak the language of the other peoples (see Nehemiah 13:24). They had even given their daughters in marriage to the other nations. How painful this must have been for Nehemiah. His original burden was to build the walls. His heart ached that the people of God should be distinctive and different. He fought against every obstacle and laboured night and day to erect the walls only to find the next generation carelessly going through the gates and committing themselves even into a marriage bond with the ungodly. What fellowship has light with darkness? How can believers be bound together with unbelievers? Believers can find common ground with unbelievers at a superficial level. They can enjoy the same music, similar books, an interest in sport; but these superficial distractions are not the rock on which to build a home. They are very much the sand that causes final heartbreak and collapse. To say that Nehemiah dealt with these issues ruthlessly is an understatement. As a true reformer his zeal knew no limits!

It's all over!

Finally, I would like to point out the way in which the book ends. Chapter 13 tells us all about the ongoing battles that will be there until the end. Then strangely, we read what seem to be very mundane words: *"I arranged for the supply of wood at appointed times and for the firstfruits. Remember me, O my God, for good"* (Nehemiah 13:31) and suddenly the book is finished! It doesn't even say that they lived happily ever after! As I contemplated this strange conclusion I asked the Lord what it meant. I felt that God told me it reminds us that we are moving swiftly to a moment when everything will suddenly end. We shall be working, as they were at the end of the book of Acts, which stops in a similar way. The book of Acts is not concluded with a flourish, recording that thousands were being swept into the kingdom in Rome. It simply says, *"*[Paul] *stayed two full years in his own rented quarters . . . preaching the kingdom of God"* (Acts 28:30–31).

One day the world is simply going to stop. It will not necessarily be on the last night of a tremendous international convention. The word will not sweep around the nations. Large conferences will not be organised with huge choirs to prepare for the end. It will be like the end of Nehemiah, who was making provision for contributions of wood. Suddenly everything is finished. You might say, "I thought there was some more!" No more! Finished! It will all suddenly be over. The Bible is very plain that this is how it will be – like a thief in the night. In the days of Noah they were marrying, buying, selling, working – suddenly, that was it! We are near to this day. No more Church history. No more world.

No more of this fleeting time. The end of this present age.
Gone!

> *"Behold, I am coming soon! My reward is with me, and I will give to everyone according to what he has done."*
>
> (Revelation 22:12 NIV)

About the Author

Terry Virgo is based at Church of Christ the King, Brighton, UK and is the founder of *Newfrontiers*, a worldwide family of nearly 500 churches. A well-known Bible teacher, Terry speaks at conferences around the world and hosts the international conference *Together on a Mission*, which draws thousands of delegates to Brighton each year.

Terry is married to Wendy and they have five grown up children.

By the Same Author

God's Lavish Grace (Monarch)
Does the Future Have a Church? (Kingsway)
No Well-Worn Paths (Kingsway)
A People Prepared (Kingsway)
Enjoying God's Grace (Kingsway)
Explaining Reigning in Life (Sovereign World)
From Refreshing to Revival (Kingsway)
God Knows You're Human (Cityhill Publishing)
Men of Destiny (Kingsway)
Praying the Lord's Prayer (Word)
Receiving the Holy Spirit and His Gifts (Word)
Restoration in the Church (Kingsway)
Start (Kingsway)
Weak People, Mighty God (Kingsway)

Newfrontiers Information

Newfrontiers is a worldwide family of churches on a mission to establish the kingdom of God by:

- restoring the Church
- making disciples
- training leaders
- planting churches

For more information please visit our web site at:

www.newfrontiers.xtn.org

or contact:

Newfrontiers
17 Clarendon Villas
Hove
East Sussex BN3 3RE
United Kingdom

Phone: (+44) 1273 234555
Fax: (+44) 1273 234556
Email: office@newfrontiers.xtn.org

We hope you enjoyed reading this New Wine book.
For details of other New Wine books
and a range of 2,000 titles from other
Word and Spirit publishers visit our website:
www.newwineministries.co.uk